BRAS

Le Bien-Etre by HC

BRAS

❧ ❧ ❧

A Private View

ROSEMARY HAWTHORNE
Author of
Knickers: An Intimate Appraisal

Drawings by Mary Want

Souvenir Press

First published in Great Britain 1992 by Souvenir Press Ltd,
43 Great Russell Street, London WC1B 3PA
and simultaneously in Canada

ISBN 0 285 63086 5

Photoset and Printed in Great Britain by
Redwood Press Limited,
Melksham, Wiltshire.

The author wishes to thank Valerie Threlfall, Jean White, Cynthia
Noble, Jean Bruce, Sue Loder, June Kenton and all the many
friends, acquaintances and costume dealers who have discovered
vintage bras for the purposes of this book.
    Also many thanks to the companies credited within these pages,
including: Warner's Ltd; Playtex, Triumph (International); Gossard
Ltd, the Marks & Spencer Organisation, Maidenform Ltd, Lovable,
Frederick's of Hollywood, Silhouette Ltd., Shannalles of London;
Janet Reger. Special thanks to Rigby and Peller for loaning the 1991
'Madonna' Corset for illustration.
    The quotations from *Cold Comfort Farm* by Stella Gibbons (©
Copyright 1932 by Stella Gibbons) are reproduced by permission of
Curtis Brown Ltd., London. A number of illustrations are repro-
duced with thanks from *Drapers' Record*, trade publication for the
fashion industry established 1887, now known as *DR The Fashion
Business*.

CONTENTS

This book is dedicated to my sons,
Seth, Giles, Jo and Seamus —
who between them know more
than they should about bras

The original garments illustrated within these pages
are from the author's collection.

PREFACE

THE SONG OF THE BRA

Busts and bosoms have I known
  Of various shapes and sizes,
From grievous disappointments
  To jubilant surprises.

Anon 1940

Bras come in many shapes and sizes — like their owners. There are big ones, small ones, oddly-shaped ones; some frivolous and fashionable, others strictly functional. They are more than just an item of supportive clothing: they symbolise eroticism, intimacy and femininity, and they also tell us a lot about the hidden nature of women and how they wish to appear and appeal. Every girl remembers the excitement of wearing her first bra — her public initiation into womanhood.

  This book is an entertainment, a small fragment of social history. I ask nothing more than that it may be read with interest and the occasional chuckle. Let those who seek deeper works go elsewhere.

  Most of us could get along quite nicely without retaining a single fact about bras. Our only concern, if we have one, is that they are still around, and indeed quite a few are bought and sold in the space of a year. They do, however, as the Mock

7

Turtle would say, have a 'history'. In less than a hundred years they have established themselves as the second most indispensable and intimate female garment.

They may not be collectors' items in the same way as snuff-boxes or Georgian caddy-spoons, but they do have a lot going for them in terms of human interest. If you want a really tell-tale picture of how women's lives have altered over the past eighty years, you can have no better guide than a representative selection of old bras, believe me.

R.H.

Brassiere, 1912. A woman's underbodice worn to support the breasts. A term used in America from 1907. Obsolete meaning in France. In French a *brassière* means an infant's underbodice. *Oxford Shorter English Dictionary*.

Larousse's French Dictionary gives the definition as 'A harness, leading strings or the shoulder straps of a rucksack'.

In France this garment is known as a *soutien-gorge* — breast supporter.

ONE
IN THE BEGINNING

And all that faith creates or love desires,
Terrible, strange, sublime and beauteous shapes.
    from *Prometheus Unbound*. Percy Bysshe Shelley

In the beginning came shape. After Eve had flung on a fig-leaf or two — most probably three — and her daughters and granddaughters had done wonders with old bear skins, succeeding generations of women became preoccupied with improving on nature's design.

Unlike any other article of dress, corsets and eventually bras were not just covers for the body or protection from the elements, but skilfully contrived devices whereby women could alter their silhouettes, adding or subtracting in those areas where Mother Nature's arithmetic had been somewhat careless. In the process they fell upon the greatest sexual catchpenny of all time; female vanity led them to show off a slim waist, and once that area had been landmarked, territories to north and south — particularly north — became vastly important.

In Ancient Crete around 1600 BC, Minoan ladies favoured a kind of boned bodice that supported their bared breasts; this advanced piece of design was lost, forgotten, like so many advanced ideas, to be rediscovered nearly four thousand years later. The women of Ancient Greece and Rome, in the third and fourth centuries BC, wore simple, sensuous, draped tunics which were caught up, banded or girdled in many different ways, but made no attempt to alter the shape beneath.

By about AD 900 European women's clothes had a shrouded form — tunics and cloaks with a strong 'religious' influence. Even as late as the twelfth century both men and women still wore flowing robes that were essentially the same undefined shape, although the waist was usually loosely girdled. Towards the end of the following century, however, things begin to change: women's clothes acquired a distinct, female shape in cut and detail, that by the fourteenth century had developed a vivid emphasis.

Beneath the elegant, close-cut tunic bodice was worn a linen smock or shift, a forerunner of the Victorian chemise, and a new garment — a stiff linen underbodice called a 'cotte' which, roughly translated, means a 'rib-sticking garment'. By the fifteenth century the 'cotte' had another name: it was known as a 'body' or, more cor-

rectly, a 'pair of bodys' since it was made in two pieces fastening back and front.

In Spain, wire and steel were used to reinforce a snappy number, afterwards referred to as the 'Spanish body'. Spain was the fashion leader of the time and dreamed up this Iron Maiden which the English adventurers, not to be outdone, pillaged and pirated back across the high seas as zealously as they did Spain's other treasures. The sixteenth century 'body' began to be strengthened with slats of wood and whalebone; it could be worn as an undergarment or, in rich and costly materials, an outer one.

In both cases it made a rigid, exacting article of

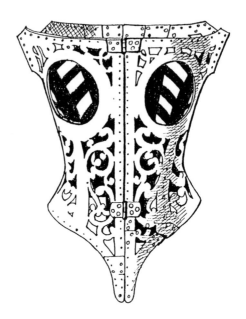

clothing. Aristocratic Tudor and, even more so, Elizabethan women knew the agony of being literally encased in wood and whalebone from high under the armpits to low on the hips. The fashionable dress bodice was a tapering tube, the front point reaching as low down as possible and just — just — allowing the wearer to sit. Slouching was neither permissible nor possible.

The 'body' was often made from leather and spiked with whalebone (which sounds about as attractive as a pair of tarpaulin knickers!). It was, of course, hot and very smelly to wear. A contemporary writer, observing all this self-inflicted torture, noted: '. . . to have a fine Hispanic body, what Gehennas do our women not suffer.'

It seems only right and proper at this juncture to mention the plight of the whale. For centuries whalebone was used as the stiffening agent in female — and male — dress. It came from the horny 'plates' or teeth of the baleen whale which may have as many as three hundred 'baleen' plates on either side of its jaw. They are approximately ten feet long and one foot wide and each one is roughly triangular in shape with one edge smooth and hard, the other bristly with fibres.

The cutting of whalebone was a tremendous industry; flexible, light whalebone replaced the iron and steel in the sixteenth century corset and was still in demand, for exactly the same purpose, in the twentieth century. A plate of baleen might be split the entire length, to any fine

measure, and not lose the peculiar characteristics so necessary to the success of a well-constructed corset. Mercifully, in the late nineteenth century,

fibre and rust-proof steels, and eventually plastic 'Flexi' bones, were introduced and whales were no longer martyrs to human vanity.

The seventeenth century was about a quarter way through when a new fashion crossed the Channel from France along with Henrietta Maria, Charles I's young wife. The uncomfortable, elongated Elizabethan torso was modified; necklines became lower and oval while skirts grew softer, lighter, and generally more graceful. Clothes were increasingly less 'stuffy', the female shape rounder, the breasts not so confined, and the 'body' changed its name to 'stays' (to 'stay the body') — a name which is still used today by many older people. I have a friend in her nineties who tells me that 'stays' were the correct, polite term from her youth; a 'corset' was trade only.

In the early centuries all the Top People's clothes for both men and women, including corsets, were cut and stitched by male tailors, but in 1675 the French tailors lost this monopoly and were forced to recognise women in a newly formed guild of lady 'mantua' or dress makers (*couturières*). From then on ladies of quality could be fitted with inner and outer clothes by members of their own sex — with the exception , that is, of corsets!

Certain male tailors — rather cleverly — took upon themselves the title of *Tailleur du Corps Balleine* (Tailor of the Whalebone Body) because they claimed that the skill and strength needed to cut and make these heavy stays were beyond the capabilities of women! For similar reasons, they also appropriated the making of coats, cloaks and riding habits, thus ensuring themselves a specialised trade with the Court and aristocracy. They were thus the forerunners of the modern bespoke men's tailors.

This male prerogative of corset-making spread throughout Europe: every town began to have its own 'body tailor'. They were the VIPs of the trade and by the eighteenth century were the butt of satirical cartoonists, who cruelly recorded the particular nature of the staymaker's job in the nice-work-if-you-can-get-it vein. The French Revolution, however, put an end to their monopoly. Their association with the Court was their undoing, and as lighter materials and improved techniques were developed, women *couturières* began to take over the corset trade

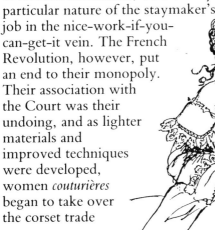

as well as dressmaking. By the time the sewing machine arrived in the 1850s, the increased business in corsetry was such that hundreds of women were employed in this area of garment-making.

Nevertheless, the eighteenth century had seen an exuberance and pleasure in dressing that has never been surpassed. It was an enriched hundred years full of wit, reason and receptive intelligence — possibly the most elegantly dressed century in history. The beauty and charm of women's clothes reached a high point of sartorial success — and the stays were magnificent. The corset shortened and could be laced either front or back — or both; the waist was strictly confined but the breasts were elevated and prominent, like two dumplings on a shelf. The overall look was captivating and extremely feminine, the tight bodices setting off the wide, full-gathered skirts.

This was still a long way from the beginning of the bra, but as the eighteenth century drew to a close there were glimmerings of an idea that would make such a garment a reality in the western world.

As it happened it took another hundred years for that reality to put in a tangible appearance.

TWO
A BRA IS BORN

Mrs Smiling's second interest was her collection of brassieres, and her search for a perfect one. She was reputed to have the largest and finest collection of these garments in the world. It was hoped that on her death it would be left to the nation.

Cold Comfort Farm. Stella Gibbons

In a sense, the bra, or something very like it, had been created long before its rapid rise to popularity in the early years of the twentieth century.

There is an ancient mosaic in Sicily showing a woman athlete wearing what appear to be a bra and briefs. In fact, the bra was called a *strophium* or *mamillare* and was made with strips of soft leather; it was worn by both Greek and Roman women who had 'physically demanding' jobs or 'over-developed' breasts.

We hear no more about anything remotely resembling a bra until the late eighteenth century, when a recreated classical 'antique' look was all the rage in fashionable western society. Then muslin frocks were mounted on linen linings, with side-pieces that crossed under the breasts and fastened, sometimes with dress pins or, more usually, with small tie tapes.

An example is mentioned in *The Book of Costume* written by 'A Lady of Rank' and published in the late nineteenth century:

> During the (French) Revolution the Athenian mode of attire was adopted. A French lady of that time gives us the following account of it: 'A simple piece of linen, slightly laced before, while it leaves the waist uncompressed, serves the purpose of a corset'.

Undoubtedly, it would have been a style scornfully dismissed by Victorian women of the 1880s and '90s. They would have considered their great-grandmothers vulgar to have 'let themselves go' in such a way; abandoned dressing went hand in hand with abandoned moral behaviour. However, Victorian moral rectitude stopped the decline into the pit and the poor old bosom had to retreat, yet again, behind whalebone barricades for another period of imprisonment until, one wonderful day in the early 1900s, a bra was born.

It happened something like this.

The bra's immediate ancestors were fine, robustly made Victorian whaleboned corsets

19

whose peerless pedigree, as we have seen, reached back through the centuries. They were tough, disciplined, alluring, dignified and utterly necessary. Superbly cut, impeccably sewn, they were triumphantly engineered aids towards that epitome of perfect womanhood — the hour-glass figure.

I have just such a corset, a fine, strong garment dating from 1860–70, made of dull black satin lined with cotton. It is heavy and close-stitched in a most complicated design and contains one hundred and four cased lengths of cording as well as twenty whalebones, which give it a good, firm shape. The steel 'busk' is front-fastening and the corset is back-laced. Short lengths of cord make a

curved basque over the hips while longer cords are channelled in bands at the back. This makes for excellent support and flexibility.

Such a corset would have been worn with the early bustle dresses.

The bra's progenitor was a lightweight by comparison. In the 1850s Victorian women, already tottering under the combined weight of whaleboned corsets, chemise, drawers and umpteen petticoats, decided to add yet another article to their laundry lists — a corset cover. Whether this was designed to protect the corset from the dress or the dress from the corset is unclear, but whatever the reason, it arrived, in the form of a short, fairly plain underbodice made of cotton or linen. I have one dating from about 1850 made of linen, with a wide neckline decorated with panels of *broderie anglaise*. It has large brass wire hooks and eyes that fasten the bodice at the front. There are neatly inserted piped seams around the sleeve heads and the whole garment is hand-sewn.

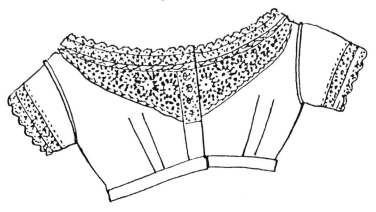

By the end of the century the corset cover's revamped image had assumed the title of 'camisole' (from the Arabic word *kamis*, meaning 'under-tunic'). This was a flighty, lace-trimmed affair, and by the time the old Queen died and her son, Edward VII, became king, it positively revelled in frills. A pretty example from this period is of fine lawn, wreathed in pin-tucks and lace insertions. A professionally sewn garment, possibly made as part of a wedding trousseau, it fastens at the front with tiny pearl buttons.

The Edwardian woman (1901–1910) was definitely mono-bosomed, with an august swell to her frontage like a roll-top desk. She was a creature who avoided any suggestion that her ample breast might be twin-souled. Under her aegis the camisole developed another important facet of its personality: by 1905 it is already described as a 'bust bodice' or, in the jargon of the time, a 'BB'.

The camisole, aka bust bodice, now had to face up to new responsibilities — namely ensuring

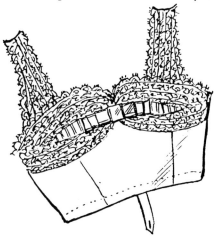

and enhancing a shapely bosom as the old corset lost its grip and, giving in to the pull of gravity once suspenders were added to its lower extremities, began to slide slowly downwards and become a mere girdle, good for nothing but flattening the buttocks and stomach and holding up stockings.

A charming bust bodice of about 1908 is made from cream silk with the yoke and shoulders in banded lace. There is a small reference to separate breasts — a bit of restrained tucking marks the spot — and the effect is modestly screened by a satin bow. This BB has pearl buttons that fasten at the back (you needed a maid or an attentive husband) and the label states that it was purchased at Woollands, Brs., 107, Knightsbridge. Bust bodices have a small tab or loop — or hook on a tape — sewn centre front. This was called the stay-hook and the device was attached to the top of the retreating corset, thus preventing total separation.

Somewhere around 1908 the bra emerged, more by accident than design, like a butterfly from the chrysalis, ready for the supporting rôle ahead. Many contemporary fashion designers held claim to having 'invented' it — they included the French seamstress and corsetière, Hermione Cadolle, Paul Poiret and the daring American 'Lucile' — but, in truth, no one is quite certain how, when or where this garment was conceived and born. It just happened — and like all great innovative designs it was simple, arriving at the right moment in history to get itself accepted into the bastions of trend-making society.

And here it is, at the dawn of a new age of undies. They certainly don't make them like this any more! You may not recognise it — but this *is* a brassiere. Stamped on the stay-strap are the words BRASSIERE. MODEL 441, BRITISH MADE.

This bra has been 'mine' for several years and I call it Sophronia, a name I consider — alongside George Bernard Shaw — to be suited to an enlightened, New Woman image. It is made of strong, twilled cotton with three ten-inch whalebones slotted into tape casings; these can be removed for washing. The wide shoulder-straps are cut as part of the whole bodice, and it fastens at the back with a large button and bring-round-the-front-tapes. The effect, when worn, is somewhat pouter pigeon.

It is not particularly pretty or subtle, its only

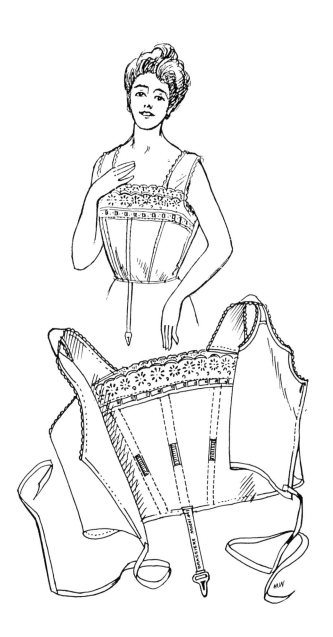

concession to femininity being an edging of *broderie anglaise* with a bit of pale pink baby ribbon slotted through it. However, this is a transitional garment, heralding the changes that were to come in the fashionable world.

Sophronia, sent to me by a woman in Dundee along with a gentleman's nightshirt and a pair of stiff cuffs, is part of history in the making — or the female shape in the re-making.

Only two or three years later the design was already lighter and less matronly. 'LA CYBELE'

(No 18 British Made) was of white cotton, still based on the bust bodice shape, with two cased whalebones and tie-front tapes. It was attractively finished with a deep band of machine-made lace.

An editorial comment in *The Lady* of 1915 sums up the ambivalent fashion front of the time: 'A pretty bust bodice or brassiere now counts for as much an essential as a corset.'

❧   ❧   ❧

The first patented bra happened on the scene by pure chance. In 1913 a young New York debutante, Mary Phelps Jacobs, was preparing to go to a dance. Mary hated the restrictive, heavy evening corsets of her time and, with the help of two handkerchiefs, pink baby ribbon and her French maid, designed what the modern world would recognise as a bra.

Mary Jacobs was a descendant of the steam boat pioneer, Richard Fulton, and in her book *The Passionate Years* she wrote: 'I believe my ardour for invention springs from his loins — I cannot say that the brassiere will ever take as great a place in history as the steam boat, but I did invent it . . .'

She made a few copies for her friends and then patented the design in 1914, under the name of Caresse Crosby, calling her invention the 'Backless Brassiere'. The product did not sell and a disillusioned Mary Jacobs sold her rights to the Warner Brothers Corset Company for $1,500. The patent was later valued at $15,000,000. She died in 1970, having seen her original, simple patent develop into a mammoth industry.

But it was this little rich girl who first devised a scanty bosom-sling that left the midriff bare and which the world now calls a bra.

Or was it her French maid?

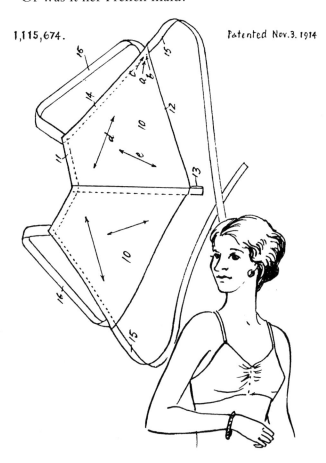

1,115,674.   Patented Nov. 3. 1914

THREE
GOING DOWN

She was an authority on the cut, fit, colour, construction and proper functioning of a brassiere...
Cold Comfort Farm. Stella Gibbons

After the 1914–18 War everything went a bit flat. Brassieres, or 'bandeaux' as they were often called at this time, became nothing more than strips of lacy material with ribbon straps. Pouter pigeons had had their day: suppression was the new-found expression of feminine beauty.

Gabrielle 'Coco' Chanel, the greatest designer of the early twentieth century, was busy convincing her Society clientele that they would not only look bewitchingly feminine and elegant in her charming little frocks, but would be comfortable as well. The shorter, simpler, straighter clothes created the need for slender, boyish figures. It was essentially a youthful look.

A FORM OF FLATTERY

You're flatter by far than Fiona,
But is Flavia flatter than me?
Can Frances, who surely is fatter,
Get away with a bosom that's free?

Fenella's a frock by Fortuny
Which is frightfully fine at the top—
You can see that her body is puny
And there's nothing to flipperty-flop.

It's fearfully fagging on figures!
Fie! Fashion's so fickle and fey.
I'm physically fraught by the feeling
That I'm flattening my frontage away.

Oh, it's fiendish unfair on a flapper,
Who's fantastically thrilled by the Vote,
To find that her female attractions
Are features no longer of note!

The bras from this period, about 1918 to the early 1920s, include some intriguing offerings. There are home-made examples like one fine white cotton bra which has very little shaping and is in effect no more than the old BB with a bit of separation. It is hand and machine sewn, with pin-tucks, and is trimmed with baby lace.

It was obviously made for a young girl and the main difficulty, as I see it, was the business of getting it on and off. There are no openings and it would have meant struggling it over your head — which surely rendered it a less than perfect fit around the bust.

Then there is a big, cotton lace wrap-around

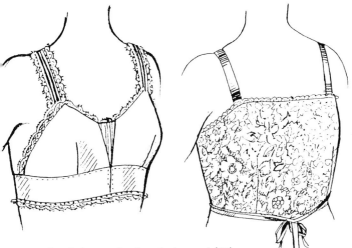

style. It is marked as being a 'dB'
brassiere on the stay-hook, which is sewn
to a large piece of elastic in the front. The lace is
lined with net and at the point where the
shoulderstraps join the back there are two small
bones inserted. There are four small bust darts
(which appear to do nothing!) and fastening is by
means of cross-over tape ties around the midriff.

Eton crops and 'no bosom, no waist' were the
symbols of the 1920s emancipated woman. Fair
enough if you hadn't got much in the way of 'the
reservoirs of maternity', as a Victorian writer
coyly referred to them. But what, oh heavens, if
you sported a massive pair of knockers? What did
you do? What *could* you do? All kinds of uncomfortable, deflating aids were sought. Tightly
binding your bosom with strips of flannel was
one way — and then you slept all night on your
tummy.

You could try dieting — lots of diets were published during the next two decades — while others had more faith and just prayed hard that their bosoms would shrivel up in the night. What was the use of the Vote if you did not have a suitably emancipated figure to go with it?

A more practical, less emotional approach was to purchase — and diligently wear — the noted Symington Side-Lacer. This was really a reinforced bust bodice made of heavy white cotton with criss-cross bands of material stitched across the front. With button front-fastening and stay strap, it was in production by 1921 but took on another, incredibly popular, lease of life in 1925 when side-lacing was added. This curious device could be tightened to flatten the breasts in an effective, fashionable way.

For Bright Young Things, however, a slight, net-lined, lace bandeau bra was more the sort of thing. Well made and cut in four horizontal sec-

tions, it had pink satin straps and a single button and loop closure at the back. An elastic loop remained in the front for attaching it to the girdle.

The only black lace bra I have from the 1920s with a flattening, or perhaps flattering, effect has a label proclaiming it to be a 'Venus' brassiere. It has a net lining and is cut in six sections which are then seamed. A set of six hook-and-eye fastenings are at the back (not easy to manage on your

Royal Acta

Ladyswear Ltd.
447 OXFORD STREET W.1
(OPPOSITE SELFRIDGES)
AND 148 BROMPTON ROAD SW3
(TWO DOORS FROM HARRODS)

own, especially if, like the Venus de Milo, you have no hands). The bra has ribbon straps with elastic 'tug' points for a non-slip fit.

One of my most fascinating finds was a bra from the late 1920s or early '30s, with the most explicit label I have ever come across. Rejoicing in the name of the 'Royal Acta', it not only boasts that it is British made but, on a second label, gives the following, detailed directions:

> Ladyswear Ltd. 447 Oxford Street, W.1
> (opposite Selfridges)
> and at 143 Brompton Road, SW3
> (two doors from Harrods)

Presumably this helped a country bumpkin on a shopping spree in town?

I think my favourite bandeau bra is one made from 'Aertex' cellular cotton. It is really large and enveloping with the usual wrap-around tapes. It also sports magnificent shoulder-straps, buttoning on back and front with a 'braces' fastening, the pearl buttons large and strong. As if this were not enough, the owner, for added assurance, has created another set of straps, this time in black silk, which also attach to large pearl buttons.

The woven label says, 'Size 44/46 Provisional Patent 14117', and on the wide stay-strap is printed, 'KRECT' Brassiere. Model 633. English Make. The strap is furnished with a hefty metal hook . . . and a safety-pin.

'Aertex' was the first cellular cotton fabric, developed in 1887, and you can see what a hold Health versus Underwear has long had on the public imagination by the assertive wording to be

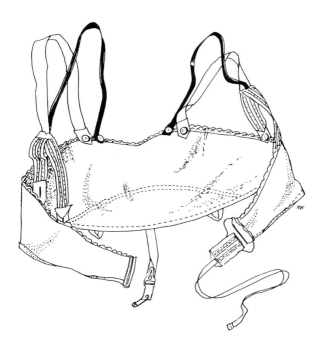

found in trade advertisements from the late nineteenth century onwards.

Dr Jaeger started the ball rolling in the late 1870s by proclaiming, with some passion, his feelings on the subject in his book *Health Culture*, in which he insisted on the positive good, for mind and body, that came from wearing wool — not only as underclothes but also as top clothes. Chemises, vests, drawers, petticoats, camisoles, corsets — right up to your pocket handkerchief and hat-band — all, in Dr Jaeger's expert opinion, should be pure, natural, undyed, unbleached wool.

Much mocking went on in the Press of the time about this gentleman's eccentric views.

'Aertex' came next, its superior wash-tub survival knocking wool back a notch or two; then the cellular cotton bandwagon was given a jolt as Empire Linen Mesh went into full-scale production.

Without doubt this product, made from pure Irish linen, was very good; the only trouble was that everyone still called it 'Aertex'. That was the name people remembered then — and still do.

❧   ❧   ❧

By the 1930s the female shape was serious business. Many great corset firms were now in existence, both at home and abroad — Warner Brothers, Triumph, Maidenform, Berlei, Twilfit, Gossard, Symingtons, Spirella — the list is endless. By this time, too, the diminutive word 'bra' had come into general use.

Since the late nineteenth century lace had made a valuable contribution towards feminine allure — particularly in the state of undress. The fine cotton textile laces manufactured between the Wars meant that corsetry designers had a good, strong surface material that not only looked very attractive but also provided the essential 'give' over the contours.

Two pretty lace bras in my collection date from this time. Both are made to reveal more natural, separated breasts. One is a long-line (waist length) bra in *écru* — a creamy fawn shade

— and is lined with fine net. It is nicely made, cut in four sections and joined with vertical inserts of coarser lace. This lace is also used to edge the bodice. The hook-and-eye fastenings are at the back and the midriff is reinforced with a strong,

pink cotton fabric. Two elastic tabs button to the girdle and the shoulder straps are made from satin ribbon. This bra looks to me as though it was made by a professional dressmaker.

The other bra is extremely pretty, made of white lace with the usual net lining, professionally machine sewn and hand-finished and cut from a Paris pattern in the mid-1930s. The woman who wore this bra was very slender, so skilful darting was used to achieve a perfectly rounded fit over the bust. It has satin shoulder straps and an elastic and button back-fastening. It was made in Egypt by a local dressmaker and was part of a complete set of underclothes for a wedding trousseau.

❦   ❦   ❦

As Rudyard Kipling says in 'How the Camel Got His Hump', 'You must *not* forget the Suspenders, Best Beloved', and although this book is about the development of the bra, from time to time I must take a look at the progress of the corset.

By the 1920s, younger women seeking to wear comfortable, less restrictive top clothes were also happy to do without rigorous corsetry. There was an element of society (generally the wealthier, educated element) whose women denied themselves the sweet torture, inflicted on their mothers, of whaleboned stays and relied on the lightweight control of loomed elastic.

Latex emulsion was the most positive discovery for the corsetry industry. The sap of rubber trees was exported from the Far East plantations in sealed drums, having first had chemical additives introduced which prevented the solution from hardening. It arrived in a perfect, gungy condition at the rubber processing factories, ready to be used in hundreds of different ways, both domestic and commercial.

The Dunlop Rubber Company's research chemists discovered a treatment that converted the raw latex solution into strong elastic thread, capable of being produced in considerable lengths and a variety of thicknesses. This was the yarn which eventually became woven or knitted elastic fabric, washable and amenable to being cut in any shape or size.

This brilliant textile, called Lastex, brought new life to the corset trade. A 'good figure' need no longer depend on bones, busks or lacing. Now elasticated materials meant that figure control was steered by the 'pull' of the yarn working within a design.

Out of this wisdom came two famous garments — and many other prototypes.

In 1925, Gossard, an American company with a London office in Regent Street and a factory at Leighton Buzzard, promoted a type of corselette known as the 'Gossard Complete'. It was a revolutionary piece of clothing. 'On in 17 seconds' ran the advertising slogan — thus making hundreds of ladies' maids redundant overnight as their mistresses no longer needed help to fasten their corsets.

Made of pink satin lined with cotton, the bust section of the 'Complete' is needlerun textile lace

lined with net. It is low backed (evening dresses were becoming 'backless' at this time) and has ribbon shoulder straps. There are Lastex side and front panels while a fourteen-strong hook-and-eye placket fastens down the left side. The four wide suspenders are covered with a deep flounce of lace and there is also a buttoned 'hinge' of net between the legs.

This remarkable and extremely forward-thinking piece of corsetry design became immensely popular and no wonder — not a whale-bone in sight and yet assuredly a fine, firm foundation garment. However, looking at the run of fourteen hooks I do wonder about the validity of the 'on in 17 seconds' claim.

The other great Lastex girdle of the period — possibly the most famous of them all — was the two-way stretch 'roll-on'. It remained a constant favourite until the 1960s when the advent of tights (and even lighter nylon yarns) rendered it obsolete.

Young girls who grew into middle-aged women wore roll-ons faithfully until they could no longer find a shop that stocked them and the English language gained a generic — 'roll-on' was synonymous with 'girdle'.

Older actresses tell me that in the 1930s and '40s a roll-on was the way to keep the boobs at bay when they played male characters in Shakespeare. Many a stalwart spear-carrier in a less than lavish provincial production had her most obvious female charms flattened beneath a roll-on undervest!

Incidentally, you may like to know that it took a hundred years to perfect narrow threading elastic and make it the nice stretchy stuff we all take for granted. The largest supplier is a family firm, Tubbs (Elastic) Ltd, who have expanded production until their output has a capacity of about one-and-a-half million metres a week. In Shakespeare's words, they have indeed 'put a girdle round the earth'.

FOUR
SEPARATE ENTITIES

... her friends had learned that her interest, even in moments of extreme emotional or physical distress, could be aroused and her composure restored by the hasty utterance of the phrase: 'I saw a brassiere today, Mary, that would have interested you...'

Cold Comfort Farm. Stella Gibbons.

By the late 1920s and early '30s, the single, most compulsive influence on fashion and female beauty was the film industry. Hollywood aroused and exuded an undeniable, almost tangible, atmosphere of glamour and sex appeal. Women who went to the cinema — the pictures, the movies, the flicks — all went home thinking how best they could copy the look that was projected by the silver screen.

This transference was of enormous value to the fashion industry in general. The beautiful actresses of the period were indeed great stars — in every sense. They had gorgeous clothes to wear, on and off the screen, and every nuance of their wardrobe was sure to be carefully noted and, if possible, copied, so that the image extended into the high street shops — or into the front room of the home dressmaker.

After years spent, in some cases, behind flannel restraints, the female breast began to smoulder for recognition. Fashion magazines decreed that the waistline re-emerge, like a long-lost friend, and emphasis, perforce, returned to the bust.

When you had the magic and
sensual enchantment of Jean
Harlow (often sewn into her satin,
bias-cut slinkies) undulating
through romantic scenes, or Mae
West, bursting to show what she
was made of, vamping a parade
of enslaved males, then a rapid
reappraisal of bras had to be
made. A natural, well-rounded
bosom was deemed the perfect
figure, so a bra was needed that
was at once sophisticated, sexy
and supportive. It also required
separation.

Rosaline Klin, a Polish-born
director of the Kestos Corsetry
Company, could not discover a
brassiere that suited either
herself or the way she felt
fashion was developing in 1927.
She started experimenting, like
Mary Jacobs before her, with a
couple of hankies (what the
bra world would have done
without hankies, I don't know).
She folded these crosswise and
joined them into one piece
with a small overlap in front.
She had, in effect, two triangles.
She sewed shoulder straps at the
top points, at the side of the
bust, and secured the other
ends at the back of the triangles.

On the back ends she attached pieces of elastic which crossed and came round to button under each breast. *Viola!* A new bra.

The Kestos bra was utterly simple — but it worked. It separated the breasts and gave them a firm, natural line. Its popularity lasted throughout the 1930s, '40s and into the early '50s. It became a generic; you didn't just go out and buy a bra — you bought a Kestos.

I have four or five Kestos bras in my collection. The one I like best is made of superb black washing silk (once more, in the 1990s, a fashionable material) and dates from around 1935. It has grey pearl buttons and adjustable shoulder straps and the label states that it is a Kestos 'High Line'.

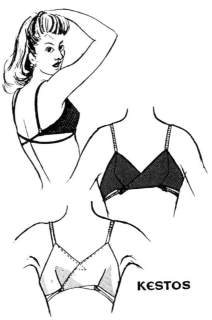

KESTOS

Another, later, Kestos (1940s) is made from shiny pink 'slipper' rayon satin, complete with 'Utility' mark. Pink rubber buttons (which tended to crack after repeated washing or, worse, mangling) fasten the elastic straps under the bust.

The Kestos is a classic piece of corsetry design showing even modern generations of designers how effective a simple arrangement of material and seaming can be.

Another beautifully made bra, from the late 1930s, is of black satin and, daringly, strapless. Briefly cut in four sections, seamed and darted to fit, it has five short bone supports —

Kestos Utility

If not quite so attractive to look at as formerly, the Kestos Utility models are still Kestos in cut and finish. The only regret that you and we have is—there can't be more of them owing to our work for the Government and wartime restrictions

Still the finest lightweight brassière

including two tiny ones let into the darts under the bust-cups (well cased!) — and an elastic and button fastening. The label is intriguing. It reads: '"Casus Lu" Mousselin. San Paulo, Rio, Copacabana, South America'. I found this one while sorting through an 'all at 25p' box in a charity shop in Bournemouth — hardly a romantic end for a bra that possibly knew exotic beginnings.

My gain entirely.

The bosom renaissance of the 1930s — despite the doldrums of economic depression (always a good sign for bosoms) — meant that the 'foundation' business was booming. Welcome news, since there had been a tremendous recession in the traditional corsetry trades during and since the Great War, and in the 1920s many larger companies had been forced to diversify into other areas of fashion and leisure wear. Some plunged into swimwear, a natural move.

By the early 1930s, however, corsetry designers were back busily working at their drawing boards and the shape of bras was mainly on their minds.

It was Warner Brothers, the vast American company, that introduced cup sizes in 1935. This great corsetry manufacturer, founded in 1874 by two doctor brothers specialising in 'Sanitary' health corsets, tumbled to the (pretty obvious) fact that women were different shapes as well as different sizes.

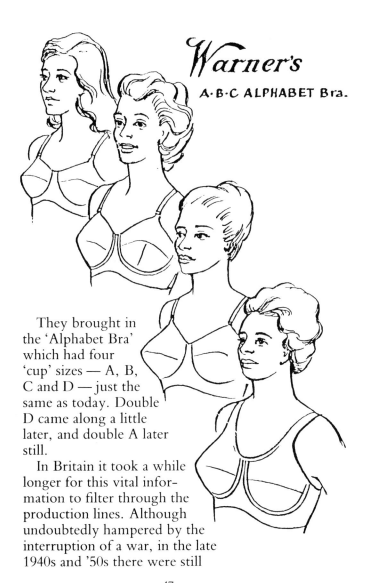

Warner's

A·B·C ALPHABET Bra.

They brought in
the 'Alphabet Bra'
which had four
'cup' sizes — A, B,
C and D — just the
same as today. Double
D came along a little
later, and double A later
still.

In Britain it took a while
longer for this vital infor-
mation to filter through the
production lines. Although
undoubtedly hampered by the
interruption of a war, in the late
1940s and '50s there were still

manufacturers labelling bust sizes with the categories Junior, Medium, Full and — wait for it — Full with Wide Waist.

The wit's way of describing those sizes was egg cup, coffee cup, tea cup and challenge cup. Which is funny so long as you're not a big girl; in which case you tend to smile bitterly and reflect that you've always had a raw deal — except, perhaps, as a handsomely 'mamillared' matron in fifth century Rome.

Warner's great series of corsetry, developed in the 1930s, was called 'Le Gant' (The Glove), a name that aptly described the close-fitting, supple and responsive garments they continued to make.

I am always particularly enchanted by the beautiful design for a trademark of a late 1930s and '40s brassiere that was produced by Warner's. Called simply 'Youth', each time I see it I am struck by the way the artist has captured the spirit of joy and freedom, the essence of youth, in this happy, silhouetted figure.

Such refreshing imagery was well in advance of its time.

FIVE
GOING UP

Mrs Smiling did not help her, because she had gone
down to the slums of Mayfair on the track of a new
kind of brassiere which she had noticed in a shop while
driving past in her car...

Cold Comfort Farm. Stella Gibbons

The Second World war brought fashion hiberna-
tion. Government restrictions came into force
and in 1941 clothing was rationed. 1942 saw the
introduction of the 'Utility' scheme whereby
every article of clothing and manufactured goods
was marked with the soon all too familiar CC41
symbol. The restrictions affected the amount of
material used when making clothes, right down
to the size, shape and number. Only a few fabrics
were manufactured — and certainly nothing
luxurious.

Undies lost all their lacy trimmings and clothes became dull, practical and uniform in appearance. Steel was urgently needed for more important things than fronting corsets and making bra hooks, and rubber, too, was commandeered for the War Effort.

To save precious coupons, 'Make-Do and Mend' became the slogan that backed up the frustrating lack of materials and kept the nation's women smiling, if a little grimly at times.

The Board of Trade invented a fictional 'Mrs Sew and Sew', a know-all who had every trick in the book concerning new ways with old gear. 'Why not make that unused chiffon evening dress into a new nightdress?' she counselled. It sounds something less than practical.

Always at their most inventive during times of hardship, women 'ran up' clothes from old curtains, bedspreads and even blackout material, which was exempt from rationing. Damaged parachutes that came into civilian hands were keenly sought to make underclothes, particularly after the War ended. Many a bra was made at home from a strip of old parachute, whether silk or nylon, and you could buy 'economy' patterns for making your own bra and knicker sets.

The magazine *Stitchcraft* even printed, in a 1945 issue, a pattern for a crochet bra — under the headline 'Get ready for the cold weather'. When made up it is surprisingly comfortable and agreeable to wear, apart from the faint trellis pattern left when you take it off.

In my collection is a peach pink cotton bra with a 'Utility' label marked 'Excelsior'. It has a well-

rusted hook (recycled scrap metal), but the rest of the bra is in good condition. Utility did not mean poorly made, rather it was skilfully designed to get the largest number of garments out of the

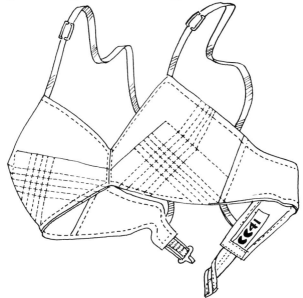

218a Walworth Road
London S.E
9th March 1947

Dear Mum,

I got the cabbage you sent, most of it is
still all right. — and the socks you knitted for
little Jim — ta everso. The baby is sleeping
through from her 10 o'clock feed. Its perishing
cold. Bills still looking for a job but the
Irish bloke next door but one has him help
on his fish round on Fridays.

I didn't know what to get our Con for her
birthday — but I got this bra off a girl
whose blokes in ladys underwear. Its no good
for me feeding baby — so I thought as how shed
like it for her bottom drawer ha, ha, since
shes walking out. Babys got a look of Bills
Mum which is a shame but shes not so sick
as little Jim was. Love,
from your Ruta xXx

cloth. This particular bra is a Cockney: she came
from a house within the sound of Bow bells.

Lots of women who can sew — even a little —
are good at 'doing something' with their clothes
if they have to, and there have been some in-
genious uses for old undies, including bras, over
the years. Not long ago someone sent me a gar-

52

net-coloured, shot silk dance dress of about 1945–50, manufactured in New York. It needed a strapless bra and it was pretty obvious that the original owner did not possess one, for she had hit upon the idea of sewing an ordinary bra, minus its shoulder straps, into the bodice of the frock. The bra label, only just visible after what appears to have been a tremendous amount of wear (she must have been a keen dancer), says that it is a 'V.G. Model' size 32.

Another oddity that came my way from the post-War years is a stripy beach outfit of bra and shorts (made from curtaining), and the bra top has an inset 'boob' holder made from the complete arm cut out of an old grandad woolly vest. It must have kept the sand out.

❦   ❦   ❦

In 1947 the French designer Christian Dior launched his New Look, and with it introduced a totally new kind of dress for women. The dull,

serviceable square-shapes that passed for clothes were eclipsed by the novel, curvy, elegant and feminine creations that stepped into the light. This fashion was instantly thrilling and inspiring to all women, sick to death as they were of the ugly, over-worn clothes that implied scarcity and evoked a memory of war. In Britain they had to curb their eagerness as — officially — material restrictions still existed (until 1952); but by that time most women had found ways of procuring a few extra coupons and a couple of 'New Look' outfits for themselves.

Since curves and femininity were back in fashion the undies also changed.

The bra changed out of all recognition.

HOW TO GET YOUR

Twilfit

....BUT PATIENCE IS REQUIRED

Twilfit Utility models represent unsurpassed value and worthily maintain the Twilfit reputation for line and finish.

As supplies are still strictly limited your best plan is to acquaint your local drapers with your requirements NOW, thus ensuring earliest possible delivery.

LEETHEMS (TWILFIT) LTD.   PORTSMOUTH

A Diversion
LIBERTY KIDS

Give me liberty, or give me death
  Speech to the Virginian Convention. Patrick Henry

Children had long worn a form of corset. In early centuries upper-class girls wore miniature versions of what their mothers wore. The higher the class of family, the earlier the child could expect to feel the constraints of whalebone. In the eighteenth century it was not uncommon for a child born to aristocratic parents to have her stays in place by the age of three or four.

By the end of the nineteenth century various lighter variations on a corset had been introduced. These were corset bodices, made in a variety of designs but generally with wide shoulder straps and a button front-fastening. Sometimes string was used instead of whalebone or, as an alternative, they could be used together.

Suspenders came into general use after 1900 but these too could be part of the corset bodice and were usually detachable. Some bodices had four buttons stitched in a diamond pattern and the buttons were utilised as follows: top button — for holding up buttonholed petticoat; two side buttons — for holding up the front and back of the drawers; bottom button — for holding a suspender.

Then, in 1908, came the famous Liberty Bodice. Symington's, a corset manufacturers established in the 1850s at Market Harborough, introduced the garment that was to become a household name. It was made from a 'new' knitted fabric reinforced with unique cloth strappings that helped maintain the shape through countless washings.

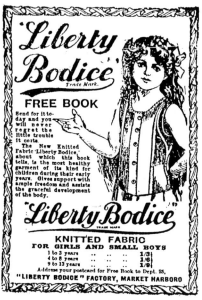

Frederick Cox, a director of Symington's, was mainly responsible for the design of the Liberty Bodice, and his young daughter, Freda, was the curly-haired model pictured in early advertisements.

At its peak there was hardly a child in the land who had not learned to button up a Liberty Bodice during the first years of life. Originally worn by both boys and girls — of all classes — it dominated infant dressing for well over fifty years. It became the essential garment in a young child's set of underclothes.

Later on, in about 1912, Symington's designed a ladies' Liberty Bodice for 'those requiring more freedom for games or other active pursuits' and these proved very popular during the First World War, but its relevance and impact was as a child's bodice. Its purpose, as ever, was to 'assist graceful development of the body' and also provide beneficial 'extra' warmth which was considered essential to healthy growth.

With its flexible, lightweight structure it was indeed a liberated piece of dress compared to earlier types of bodice. As an article of clothing it was dearly loved by mothers, nannies, aunties and other responsible grown-ups, but I fear it was loathed and detested by those who, like me, had to wear one.

Central heating eventually saw it off. Somewhere between 1965 and the early 1970s it became obsolete, but to those of us who remember its hard rubber buttons between our fingers and its clinging softness next to our skins on a cold winter's day, it is the very essence of childhood. Just to catch sight of a bodice immediately puts us in touch with the days of early nurture — a warm, nostalgic mix of 'Viyella' nightclothes, lisle stockings, coal fires, 'Ovaltine', 'Children's Hour' with Uncle Mac and the strong, pervasive smell of camphorated oil.

Believe me, there are still an awful lot of us around with that confused memory tucked away.

SIX
STILL RISING

It was no use to me. It was just a variation on the
'Venus' design made by Waber Brothers in 1938; it had
three elastic sections in front, instead of two, as I'd
hoped, and I have it already in my collection.
Cold Comfort Farm. Stella Gibbons

Some of the most engaging, amusing and extraordinary bras come from the late 1940s and '50s.
Those made in the United States and France,
particularly, were superb. Helped by the resur-
gent film industry, the bra moved in confident
ascent, reaching a pinnacle of success in the
1950s.

To a whole generation of men and women, the
Hollywood film actress Lana Turner became
known as the 'Sweater Girl'. Her cone-shaped
breasts were to become the best known, most
pinned-up projectiles in the business. Jane Russell
was another twin-turboed star who added to bra-
mania by having her outstanding bosom clad in a
bra designed for her by the aeronautical engineer
Howard Hughes, for her part in the 1943 film
The Outlaw. Proportions of such grandeur had to
be accurately assessed and a mini-construction
job was done on Miss Russell's cantilevered bra.
Harold Robbins used this colourful piece of
American history in his novel *The Carpet Baggers*.
Marilyn Monroe, Brigitte Bardot and Elizabeth
Taylor all boasted enviable cleavage, besides
other filmic attributes.

Fashion kept abreast; marketing boosted the female bosom from every angle. There was certainly nothing 'natural'-looking about the 'New Elizabethan' figure. Anyone was at liberty to see the artifice beneath the twin set — two sharp peaks that looked for all the world as though they might bore through the surface material.

This was to be the heyday of the upholstered bra. There is more than a hint of revival as I write, but nothing to match the brilliance of the high street coverage that was laid before us in the Great Bra Period.

One of the finest American bra manufacturers to flourish in the 1950s was Maidenform. This company was started by dressmakers William and Ida Rosenthal when, in the 1920s, they were prophetic enough to see that the bras they gave away as flattering accompaniments to the dresses they sold were creating more demand than the frocks. The secret of the first Maidenform bra seems to have been that instead of binding and suppressing the breasts, it separated and uplifted them. The Rosenthals had struck gold: their bras were among the brand leaders throughout the 1950s and remain so today.

French designs, as so often, were significantly ahead of their time. I have a size 32 bra of about 1950, called 'La Varecta', a charming, black net, sheer-effect affair which, with its elegant simplicity and sensual appeal, could easily be a contemporary garment. It is discreetly and cleverly cut out of four sections of material with a 'U'-shaped, cased metal hinge at the cleavage. The satin shoulder straps have elastic 'tug' points and

I dreamed we came from the U.S.A. in our *maidenform bras....*

the bra fastens at the back with a wide elastic tab and two small black buttons. It is extremely well made, a beautiful bra, with its original Harrods stock label still attached.

Many of these wonderful whirlpool-stitched 1950s bras have outstanding, emotive names — a

O wonderful wonderful, at last. . . . she cried
It was what she had always longed for.
It was prettier than salt-sea-green emeralds,
more perfect than pearls, rounder than wave-stroked pebbles.
It was new as the slim crescent moon.

It was a jewel . . . above all others.
And it was *hers*. Her treasure.
To uplift her heart.
To carry her, in all the pride of her beauty,
to magical places.
To gilt-edged invitations,
to midnight masquerades and wild beach balls.

She shimmered in its white foam embrace,
gentle and close as a lover's arms around her.
She shivered with delight in her new beauty
in her very own, very beautiful bra. Her Playtex.

good name and a good advertisement could sell a bra, then as now. There was the 'Bonfire' bra, promising to make you 'more sensational and comfortable'; 'Lovable' by Pagan, whose white rayon is now marred by brown age spots; and 'Roman Follies', stunning in black cotton with an elasticated centre panel for a really close fit.

My favourite old bra has such character that I am always enchanted by the sight of her! She slips out of her original cellophane packet (she was never worn) which is marked Medium Cup, and as she does so there is an unmistakable rubbery smell (lots of latex being used in bra manufacture in the 1950s). She is only a modest size 32 — but what a chassis!

61

Under the white cotton the rubber reinforcement is so strong that you have to knock the cups into shape with a fist. They spring instantly to attention. The cups are cut in three sections and then whirlpool-stitched, and the perfect, pointed contours are given more support by over-locking along the seams where the sections join. The effect is like a couple of cone-shaped suction cups. There is a small elastic front panel and adjustable cotton shoulder straps, and an elastic with hook fastening. The label reads: 'St. Michael. Patent applied for', and the original swing label is still attached, proclaiming, 'Inter-lined cups. Moulds to your figure'.

This bra would undoubtedly make an impression wherever she went.

A bra with a less pleasing appearance was produced by Formfit whose slogan was 'Styled in America'. It is a stylish though heavily uphol-stered affair made of machine-embroidered cotton with stiff elastic side panels. The shoulder straps are adjustable and also made of cotton. It has bust cups cut in three sections and latex lined, with four 'Flexi' plastic bones running vertically through the cups. Thus the shape remains — whether a girl is inside or no. The bra is dis-armingly named 'Confidential' — but you must believe me when I say that there is nothing confi-dential about it: it positively shouts 'tits' at you.

❧   ❧   ❧

One of the commonest colours to be found in pre-War and post-War undies is pink, usually of a

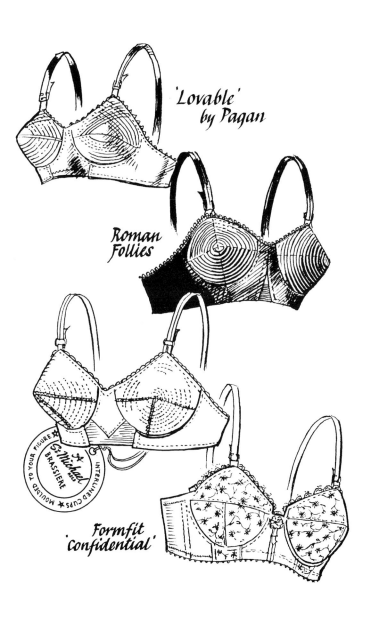

'Lovable'
by Pagan

Roman
Follies

Formfit
'Confidential'

St Michael
BRASSIERE
INTERLINED CUPS
MOULDED TO YOUR FIGURE

particularly peachy tone. Lots and lots of bras, corsets, knickers, vests and slips were made in this strangely unflattering colour.

Some years ago I bought two examples of post-War pink bras in an 'old costume' shop. I

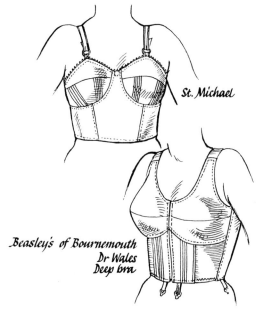

St. Michael

Beasley's of Bournemouth
Dr Wales
Deep bra

couldn't resist the lure of lustrous pearly pink glowing from cotton-backed satin. These were real heavy duty 'deep' bras, bust supporters rather than just 'fashion' garments, designed to do a tough job really well. One looked as though it had never been worn — maybe it was uncomfortable or did not fit properly, or maybe, like so many bras, it just got shoved to the back of the drawer and forgotten.

The link between 'foundation' and 'fashion' was considered of utmost importance during the decade. Beasley's, the retailer of the Dr Wales Deep Bra, was a well-known specialist corsetry shop where customers could be fitted for bespoke garments by trained fitters. They tended to deal with more matronly, conservative women who still relied on 'proper', well fitted foundation garments to control their figures and do justice to their clothes. Another firm which placed great emphasis on correct fit was 'Berlei', who were Associate Members of the Incorporated Society of London Designers. Fashion houses such as Matita, Rembrandt, Susan Small, Dereta, Hebe Sports and Lady in Black would have shown their model suits and gowns on mannequins already encased in excellent Berlei underpinnings.

SEVEN
BOSOM FRIENDS

Let her and Falsehood grapple; who ever knew Truth
put to the worse, in a free and open encounter.
Areopagitica. John Milton

A Cockney skipping song for doing the Bumps:

IRENE'S MUM

Irene's Mum says I's too skinny
To catch a man and cook his dinny.

Irene's Mum says I's too thin
To grab a bloke and live-in-sin.

Irene's Mum says I's too flat
To get a bloke in his wedding hat.

Irene's Mum says, 'You'll be bumper,
Stuff some falsies up yer jumper.'

In this story of shape and consequent development, there is another, underlying story, full of cunning deceit and artifice. It seems there is no trickery too low to which women will not stoop in pursuit of a comely figure.

In the 'Going Up' brigade there have been the most incredible and varied means of support — so much so that in 1791 *The Morning Herald* was driven to comment:

> The bosom, which Nature planted at the bottom of her chest, is pushed up by means of wadding and whalebone to a station so near her chin that, in a very full subject, that feature is sometimes lost between the invading mounds.

And in 1799 *The Times* correspondent remarked, 'The fashion for false bosoms has at least this utility — that it compels our fashionable fair to wear *something.*'

Small wonder these wags let rip in print: by the end of the eighteenth century an array of artificial aids to uplift had been introduced. These included a quilted pad that tied round under the bosom, called a 'Bolster', and a complete moulded front made of wax, dubbed 'Bosom Friends' — specifically designed to gratify the male glances at the décolleté muslin gowns of the period. This fashion was particularly cruel for older women or girls with 'thin' chests. Imagine the problems when the wax began to melt!

The nineteenth century gave *Punch* the chance to join in the fun. 'The many falsehoods made

from buckram, wool and wadding . . .' wrote one well-informed spy. In 1847 *The Lady's Newspaper*, a caring, respectable magazine for gentlewomen, carried advertisements for 'Bust Improvers' and 'Lemon Bosoms': 'The registered Bust Improver, of an air-proof material; an improvement on the pads of wool and cotton hitherto used.'

Patent Bolsters' from Gillray's cartoon 1791

The False Bosom c. 1800 dubbed Bosom Friend

The 'Lemon Bosom' was an amazing construction made from a light coiled spring in each cup, packed with bleached horsehair, contained in a pouch of whalebone-supported cotton. At the back it resembled a lemon cut lengthwise, hence its name.

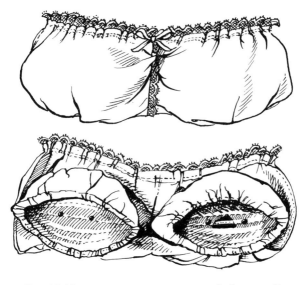

By 1860, a patent was granted for an 'improved, inflated, *undulating* artificial bust'. One can only imagine such a marvel, and also wonder at the French company of 1867 who were advertising *poitrines adherentes* of *pink rubber*. These were said to follow the 'movements of respiration with mathematical and perfect precision'.

How exciting.

Another trade advertisement of 1877 has the following goodies to recommend:

A BOSOM SECRET. Buy a pair of Main-
tenon corsets, fitting your waist measure.
The other parts of the corset will be propor-
tioned AS YOU OUGHT TO BE. Put the
corset on, and fill the vacant spaces with fine
jewellers' wool, then tack on a piece of soft
silk or cambric over the bust, thus formed to
keep the wool in place, renewing it as often
as required.

I fear this would have been a rather awkward aid
to beauty.

Bust improvers were still going from strength
to strength in the 1880s. They were worn under
the camisole and advertised as 'giving roundness
to those who are too slim'. In 1887, they came
formed as wire, cup-shaped structures or — a
simpler idea — a shaped piece of material with
circular pockets, not unlike handkerchief sachets,
into which pads of 'assorted' sizes could be
inserted.

This is still a trick used in the manufacture of some modern bras.

Victorian prudery did not jib at the discreet padding of dress bodices — particularly wedding dresses! This artful device is continually found on dresses from between 1865 to 1900, when an hour-glass figure was fashionable.

Home Chat, an upper-class magazine of the 1890s, advised worried readers on the remedy for 'thin' busts and by the early 1900s 'amplifiers' was the descriptive word used for the stiff, starched frills that fronted certain camisoles.

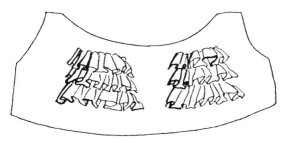

These were seen as the answer to a maiden's prayer. They could, if necessary, have the added sophistication of a braided wire edge — but this sounds far from huggable.

Above all, it is an advertisement of 1902 that compels our attention:

The PATENT BUST IMPROVER: placing possession of a bust MODELLED on that of the famous VENUS DE MILO . . . at the possession of every lady; of flesh-coloured material and less than 2ozs in weight. 7/6d (47^1/2p) a pair.

The Neene Bust Improver of 1905 went one stage further: made from 'cup-shaped, perforated metal discs weighing only ³/₄oz the pair.' The wonders of science! No price is included but it is possible they could have doubled as tea strainers — so a bargain at any price.

From that date the enthusiasm for 'going up' seems to have subsided until, with the return of the bosom culture in the 1930s, '40s and '50s, we get another good crop of imposters with a series of foam rubber pretences variously called cuties, falsies, shapelies, cheaters or gay deceivers.

It was in 1947, the year of the 'New Look', that Frederick Mellinger, an American designer, established his racy underwear company, Frederick's of Hollywood. This firm was dedicated to 'fixing flat and falling bosoms'. To this end, Mr Frederick introduced foam-rubber falsies to cope with the demand for bigger boobs. He also designed an 'Inflatable Bra', and many bras of this type were successfully marketed as a 'glamour' product in both America and France. During the 1950s and early '60s there were still bras being advertised which had 'blow-up' air pockets within their structure. From what I have been told, they were not at all reliable, being apt to spring a leak and 'whistle' air or, rumour had it, explode at high altitudes.

So, apart from resorting to drastic surgery and expensive silicone implants (upon the wisdom of which recent medical research has cast doubts), is there anything that women have not tested and tried in the diligent search for a fair and shapely bosom? I guess not.

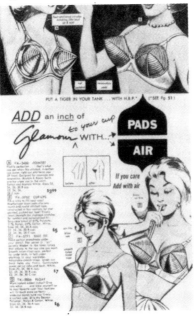

Let me end this revelation on female vanity with a story that came from a woman I met at a WI meeting where I had been talking about 1930s clothes:

One evening, before the War, I was asked out to a dance at a local hotel by a very nice young man that I'd had my eye on for some time. It was in the days when evening dresses were very low-cut or strapless. I had to borrow my sister's dress; she worked in London and bought very smart clothes. I also needed to borrow her strapless bra that, unfortunately, didn't fit me very well since I had hardly any bust to speak of.

Anyway, my sister said, 'Not to worry, you can stuff yourself out with cotton-wool and no one will be any the wiser.' This I did, and sallied forth to the dance with my new date, confident that my dress looked smashing and my shape impressive.

All was well until, near the end of the dance, I suddenly caught my boyfriend gazing curiously at my front. I glanced down, and imagine my horror when I spied mounds of cotton-wool seeping over the edge of my bodice!

Hot with embarrassment, I fled into the Ladies and remained there until it was time to go home.

However, the story had a happy ending. The following week she went out with her chap again, minus the padding, and in the goodness of time they ended up husband and wife.

As I left the hall she remarked, 'Be sure your sins will always find you out, Mrs Hawthorne! But it was the start of a happy marriage; we often have a laugh about the old cotton-wool!'

EIGHT
NO VISIBLE MEANS
OF SUPPORT

It is in evening dress that our women have reached the minimum of dress and the maximum of brass.

Social comment of 1870

The strapless bra is an incredible structure. Introduced in the 1930s, it was twenty years later, in the 1950s, that it made its mark. In the re-establishing years after the War, with an economy trying to stabilise itself and families beginning to get back to 'normal', people began to pick up the social activities of a pre-War life.

Romance was in the air, and the habit of getting dressed up and going out for the evening was revived. Even a trip to the cinema was worthy of thoughtful dressing. A new Doris Day film had you thinking in terms of gingham shirtwaisters, while an Ava Gardener demanded more obvious sophistication.

Evening dresses, whether they were 'ballerina' length or long, were full-skirted with close-fitting bodices and small waists. Wide 'shawl-collared' dresses were at first popular and then designers went the whole way and the shoulders were left completely bare.

There was an immediate need for strapless bras — particularly the supported longline type. These were refinements of the pre-War type, of which I have one in pink lace, lined with fine net and containing six cased plastic bones (now sometimes called ribs). It has a shaped 'waistcoat' edge and a gathering tape which, when pulled taut, separates the cups and 'bows' them into shape. When it is not gathered it is difficult to tell which is the top and which the bottom. It is a very simple design, but it is a good bra.

Lily of France produced an impressive bra in the late 1950s, made of pink 'Perlon' (a filmy,

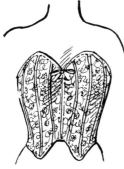

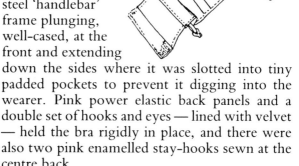

slightly opaque nylon) and lace. It had a deep-cleavaged, 'overwired' design, the continuous steel 'handlebar' frame plunging, well-cased, at the front and extending down the sides where it was slotted into tiny padded pockets to prevent it digging into the wearer. Pink power elastic back panels and a double set of hooks and eyes — lined with velvet — held the bra rigidly in place, and there were also two pink enamelled stay-hooks sewn at the centre back.

Another 'Perlon' bra — this time white and with a stern 'DON'T IRON' warning on the inside label — had defined circular stitched cups, underwired and cased in velvet lined with latex, perforated so that the air could circulate! Even so, it now has a pungent, rubbery smell when it is unpacked. It was called 'Odette', and was made by Triumph in about 1955.

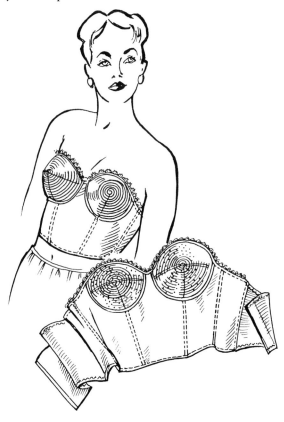

The choice available in the high street shops was amazing. One bra, designed in black satin, had the curious look of lizard skin! It was cut in nine sections, the cups forming two of the sections which had longer, cased bones to 'front up' the bodice. It was very snug fitting with an extreme 'wasp' waist and the hook-and-eye fastening was sewn into deep elastic panels at the back.

The rather weird 'lizardy' look was achieved by reinforcing the bust cups with criss-cross

stitching over the surface of the material, making it feel a trifle crêpy. It was a striking garment, made by a most famous manufacturer of the 1950s, 'English Rose'.

Formfit had a bra winsomely labelled 'Romance' that was made of white nylon, machine embroidered, with a small rosette of blue baby ribbon at the cleavage. Well cut in ten pieces with inserted panels of elastic yarn, it was exceedingly pinch-fitting and looked as disciplining as the original Spanish body. Nylon voile lined the whirlpool-stitched cups, which were underwired and had two long, sickle-shaped plastic bones inserted vertically through the centre of each. The bra in my collection is labelled size 34 but it looks far more impressive.

There were also brief strapless bras produced in quantities, and owing to the problem of actually holding them up, fascinating designs were created to try and overcome, and if possible defy,

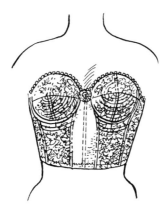

gravity. For a really inspired notion it would be hard to beat the cathedral bras! I have two, both made from sheer nylon fabric, and the white one, which is a true short strapless bra, held up by merit of designer ingenuity and tight elastic, is a real stunner. It has satin-bound edges and machine embroidery under the bust cups; the fastening is by hook on a strong tab of elastic. It is called 'Celebrity', made by Everlastik.

The most amazing feature is the four cased

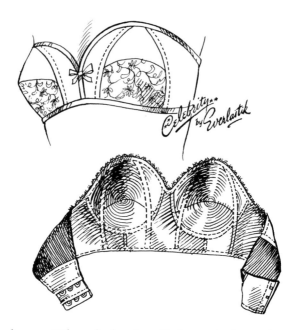

bones. When the bra is pulled taut the bones jump apart and form Gothic-shaped arches over the breasts.

The other, deeper, cathedral bra is a dark bronze colour with side panels of black elastic. Although circular stitched, it also has the arched support through the cups. It is a beautifully constructed bra with, alas, no label to identify it. I am under the impression that it is of French manufacture, but sadly, the woman who gave it to me could not remember where she had bought it. All she said was, 'It's hardly been worn because it was so uncomfortable.' The times I have heard that!

❦　　❦　　❦

Another type of long-line bra was the corset bra, or basque (extending just over the curve of the hips). It had class and a touch of drama, but not for its wearer the rock 'n' rolling at the local dance hall — she would have been to a smart cocktail party before the theatre and then on to a candlelit dinner for two. This is the shape that lined the expensive little black dress and held 15 denier stockings, straight-seamed, against sleek legs.

Evening underwear was often described with romantic, evocative names conveying a picture of wine, women and post-Edwardian lusciousness. Warner Brothers had a series called 'The Merry Widow', and I have a superb example made from black nylon voile with insertions of black lace. The cups are underwired and half-lined with latex. Two satin-cased bones rise into the base of the cups and there are nine other bones of varying lengths. The back is controlled by power-net elastic panels and there is a seven-inch long hook-and-eye fastening. The detachable suspenders are black enamel with black satin tabs.

The 'Merry Widow' was produced to coincide with the 1952 film of the same name, starring Lana Turner, and the original 'Merry Widow' foundation, worn by Miss Turner, was a full-length corselette. This was cut with attractive panels of black and white lace, incorporating slim panels of black elastic yarn net. A heavy-duty zip was inserted behind a velvet-backed, hook-and-eye flange and the whole garment was lined with nylon voile. Nine long spiral wires were cased in black satin. It was a terrific garment!

Lana Turner is reputed to have said, 'I'm telling you — the "Merry Widow" was designed by a man. A woman would never do that to another woman!'

To this day 'Merry Widow' is the generic for a corselette bra in the United States.

NINE
SWING, SIXTIES, SWING

At the opera, a gentleman was overheard to remark to another: 'Did you ever see such a thing?'
'Not since I was weaned!' came the reply.

Although it started slowly, the fashionable female shape was to undergo a distinct change during the 1960s.

Generally speaking, at the beginning of the decade fashion was still concerned with the hour-glass figure, with bra manufacturers using the boom in sales of women's magazines to put their message across.

'Youthful' was the inspirational buzz word of the early '60s. Whereas before, women dressed more or less like their mums, some now dared to wear clothes more like their teenage daughters. The Beatles, the Pill, the Mini-Cooper and the Moon all came to hand during the 1960s. On reflection it seems to have been a curious, fraught decade, full of marvellous advantages for the young, as well as a sea of uncharted social dangers.

Clothes present the same picture. The 1960s fashions caused dismay and confusion amongst many women. The over thirty-fives felt they were *just* too old (or hadn't the guts) to tackle the brevity of the mini skirt when it arrived, and older women regarded the entire look of the decade as something completely alien.

True, a skirt which came to a fourteen-inch stop, waist to thigh — as in the late 1960s — could be construed, in any language, as 'asking for it', and lots of lovely, maturer ladies declined to risk their neighbours' gossip. They compromised and turned their hems up *just* above the knee.

Their daughters, however, had no such scruples. They loved the brief skirts and so did their boyfriends. The British designer Mary Quant was the innovative Queen of the Mini, and she also created a range of bras and girdles for 'Youthlines', called 'Q Form', in 'girl-loving Lycra' (complete with the famous Quant daisies) in a 'new' colour — described as 'Barely Brown'. It was a time to be young and free, and older women had to suffer quiet outrage while the fashion industry and the admen set their eyes firmly on youth. Youth was the marketing target and the aim was to get those kids to spend the wages of full employment. It was the under twenty-fives' earnings that kept the wheels of the garment industry turning so satisfactorily — particularly in underwear and hosiery.

Looking through a copy of *She* magazine of 1965, I am struck by the number of major bra manufacturers advertising their respective wares — there are ten or more — all pushing out some pretty persuasive copy alongside their bras.

Formfit has one that is 'magically simple' and advances an 'enviable new loveliness'; Exquisite Form 'keeps you in place'; Lovable's is 'straight from Heaven . . . Cloud 7' and 'padded ever-so-lightly'; Silhouette has control that 'smuggles years off your figure' while 'Miss Twilfit' offers

'Next to Nothing' in sheer Bri-nylon.

Such blatant pleadings are possibly hard to resist.

As the 1960s drew to a close the 'look' began to concentrate on legs, and the rest of the female anatomy became almost insignificant. Narrow, childish shoulders, ant hips, and yards of match-stick legs — this child-woman was the icon of the decade.

American panti-hose or tights took over the stocking market when the inelegant gap between the stocking top and knicker bottom, with suspenders somewhere in between, became impossible to hide under tiny skirts. Girdles and suspenders found themselves carted off with the rubbish and rear ends came into

The beautiful new bra
that gives you that
youthful free-as-air feeling

YOUNG
YOU

by

Silhouette

Elastic net panels round each cup expand and contract as you breathe . . . as you move. Yet the bra stays snug — no bulging, no gaping. 'Keep-Shape' cups, lined with wafer-thin foam, mould you beautifully in a firm youthful line. With soft plush elastic back. White or Black Bri-Nylon. 32″A to 36″B cup. Also with unique insets in place of foam lining, giving lovely uplift. 32″A to 38″C cup. Both styles **19/11**. And to give shape to the *very* small bust, AAA cup 32″ to 36″. 21/-

And for diaphragm control, LONG LINE 'U' in white or black. 39/6

SILHOUETTE 'U' FOUNDATIONS, A DIVISION OF CORSETS SILHOUETTE LTD.
MAKERS OF THE FAMOUS **little X** RANGE OF FOUNDATION GARMENTS

view — some distinctly more attractive than others.

This caused consternation, if not panic, in the boardrooms of traditional corset manufacturers! Corsets were being shed left, right and centre — and the bra came in for a bit of readjustment, too. The fashion model Twiggy, as a size 6, showed us that to be very small up front was twice as beautiful, and that girls who grew neat little apples under their skinny-rib jumpers could be considered the lucky ones.

This was all so reminiscent of the 1920s.

Then the American space-age designer Rudi Gernreich scorched the ground by producing a topless swimsuit (1964). This was powerful, emotive stuff, and for a few seasons Paris *couture* played with discreetly veiled nudity on the cat-walks. Gernreich had then gone on to design the 'No Bra' bra, made of fine, sheer, stretch netting, for those that jibbed at total bra-lessness, and Warner's developed the idea further in 1965 by manufacturing a transparent bodystocking. The illusion was a nude body — in fact, it was a fairly well clad one.

Another cannon had been fired in the name of fashionable progress.

However, there was still an awful lot of traditional corsetry around in the 1960s. Fashion moved more slowly than now and the majestic 'Spirella' long-line bra in my collection, from about 1964, says it all.

Spirella was a famous firm of corset manufacturers, established in Letchworth in 1901. They specialised in a personal made-to-measure service and trained their lady fitters to go and measure their customers in the privacy of their homes. It was something of a social cachet to have a Spirella lady visit you on a bespoke mission of corsetry. I remember seeing the 'Spirella' card set up in front room windows, advertising the fact that the occupant was a trained *corsetière*, awaiting your most demanding order.

**made-to-measure
fashion service in
your home**

My Spirella bra — robust and well made as would be expected, was sent to me by a woman who enclosed with it a letter explaining the ins and outs of its making:

You will see that I used to have extra strong hooks put on and a third row of extra strong eyes. This was because I wore them so tight that both hooks and eyes were quickly distorted or ripped off altogether. In fact, I have at some time cut off the third row of

eyes, probably because they were all broken
. . . the hooks don't look too healthy, either!

My fitter very often had the greatest difficulty in fastening a new bra on me and stood
in disbelief at the 'pain' I was prepared to
endure wearing foundation garments which
were so tight . . . but, in those days, pride
had to be more than just a pinch! And
although it was against my fitter's professional principles to sell such a basically
bad-fitting garment, she also realised that
the 'customer is always right' and gave in
gracefully.

This longline bra is made from black, satin-look nylon with side panels of heavy duty, woven 'power' elastic. The shoulder straps are wide nylon with non-slip buckles. The bra is decorated with a black lace trim and nine 'spiral' stay-bones are cased into the seams. These were introduced by Spirella and, of course, are the inspiration for their name.

Recently the mother of one of my daughter's friends had a 'New Year, Good Riddance' clear-out of her extensive and, it appears, expensive wardrobe and cast aside two pearls of garment history which she passed on to me. They had been bought thirty years ago as part of her fashionable wedding trousseau. I dubbed them 'Gin' and 'Jag' because they seemed to represent the slightly 'flash' trappings of the up-to-the-minute good life of the 1960s — young executive, high life, expense account living, Art and the Adman giving old Mother Nature one hell of a boost. Plastic money enabled the Joneses to climb higher, quicker, up the social ladder.

Both these bras are French — purchased at Harrods. They are definitely 'evening' bras; certainly, you could wear them during the day, but somehow it wouldn't be right! Both are made by the same company, Scandale, and they have that combined air of superiority and sexiness that is imbued in all good French clothes.

The strapless, long-line bra is made of nylon and Lycra. Black lace is laid over the dull, pinky mauve lining. There are seven cased bones and hard, pre-formed cups with extremely resilient underwiring. A welt of wide elastic clinches the

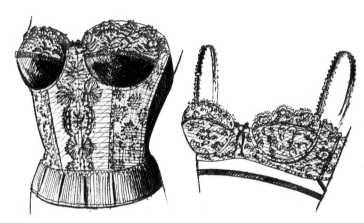

waist and a strong hook-and-eye back fastening completes a most attractive bra. The whole thing is so stiff that it can stand up unaided!

The other bra, a brief one, is made from black nylon lace over pale pink net, the bust cups firmly underwired and half-lined with shaped foam. There is a large pearl stud sewn on a black satin bow at the cleavage. Shoulder straps are combined lace and elastic and there is a complicated back fastening — a large hook on a double elastic strap with another loop of elastic encircling the rib-cage. This arrangement allowed for the straps to be 'hooked' away out of sight under the lowest of plunge-back evening dresses.

One bra in my collection is an example of the early 1960s bra-maker's art, and remained unsurpassed for decades. By 'Lovable', it has 'built-in' emphasis — pre-formed, latex-backed cups creating two boldly rounded contours that are actually more natural-looking than the twin peaks of the 1950s — though they go 'plunk'

when pushed into shape! Underwired with soft, winsey casings, the outside material is white embroidered cotton. It has a hook-and-eye fastening attached to very wide elastic side-pieces. The straps are made from cotton, with detachable

non-slip buckles and two different 'setting' po-
sitions — eminently sensible and an innovation in
1963 when this bra was bought.

It was originally worn as a strapless bra and the
woman who gave it to me said that it was bought
to go under a low-necked, low-backed dance
dress (so many new shape bras are bought for
'dress up' occasions). Although it made the dress
look superb it was actually most uncomfortable
to wear and she never felt 'nice' in it; conse-
quently it was never worn again. I wonder how
many other bras have been given the brush-off
after a one night stand, and sit patiently at the
back of a drawer awaiting another special assign-
ment — or a costume collector — to relieve their
boredom.

❦   ❦   ❦

No book about bras would be complete without
a mention of Marks & Spencer. The story of how
the company began has almost passed into
legend, but it is well worth repeating.

Michael Marks, born in 1859, the founder of
Marks & Spencer, was a refugee from Lithuania.
His family suffered many deprivations as Jews
under the Czar, and following the latter's as-
sassination Michael Marks fled the country, arriving in England in 1883.

The next year he obtained £5 credit from a
wholesaler of 'smallwares' to obtain stock from
the warehouse. Marks started trading, from a
tray round his neck, in the small villages around
Leeds. He had a sign written, saying: 'Don't ask

the price, it's a penny.' This got over the language problem and provided an excellent marketing slogan.

Soon Marks opened a market stall in Leeds. The business prospered and in 1894 he sought a partner who could provide capital for further expansion — so Thomas Spencer enters the scene and from rags to rich rags moves the story.

By 1901 the partners had 24 places in market halls and twelve shops. Michael Marks died in 1907 and the next generation, sons Simon Marks and Tom Spencer, Jr, joined the board in 1911. Simon Marks had a great friend at school, Israel Sieff; they married each other's sisters and their friendship and business acumen shaped the modern image of Marks & Spencer before Simon Marks died in 1964.

The famous 'St Michael' trademark was registered in 1928. The name was derived from St Margaret, the trade name of Corah's, one of the company's biggest garment suppliers. It was Simon's tribute to his father's memory.

Marks & Spencer is still the most successful merchandising company in the British Isles and its sales of women's underclothes are reputed to be 34 per cent of the whole market. One in three women wears an M&S bra . . . that's an awful lot of bust cups!

Those are the vital statistics that really matter.

Another company with an enormous reputation as corset-makers is Gossard. H. W. Gossard, an American firm, was founded at the turn of the century. They opened their first London office in 1921 and in 1925 introduced the aforementioned 'Gossard Complete'. They became a British Public Company in the early 1930s.

In the 1960s Gossard, along with other manufacturers, began to feel the wind of change whistling round their products. Suspenders and girdles were becoming defunct with the advent of tights; things were not as Mum had known them.

They decided to take a big chance and go for the top. They put all their money, experience and design expertise behind one bra — the 'Wonderbra'. It was launched amid a big advertising and marketing campaign in 1968. A brave gamble — and it paid off: it is still one of the world's best-selling bras.

I have four 'Wonderbras' in my collection. Two are 'as nature intended'; the others have discreet, padded interiors.

The 'Wonderbra' is a half-bra, the bosom held and prettily exposed at the top. An actress friend of mine always called them her 'cup cakes'!

All four bras are cut in the same way, in three sections of lace, and underwired, the cups slanting towards the centre. It is a very attractive and effective design and was undoubtedly the fore-runner of many similar half-bras: they are decidedly in the 'round 'em up and head 'em out' mould. Wonderbra One is made from black lace, half-lined with nylon, while plastic-covered

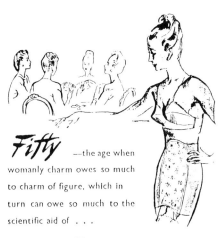

'wires', cased in brushed nylon, are slotted through under the cups. There is a ribbon hinge at the cleavage. (Many a time has a wretched wire like those worked its way loose and entered the innards of the washing machine — with dire results.)

Wonderbra Two is a really super-duper affair. It is again lace — an extraordinary orangey-pink colour with small flecks of brown. It looks rather like tinned salmon, but it is a particularly fine example of a 'Wonderbra', in pristine condition (another of those 'special occasion' bras), and is padded with small, almost secret compartments

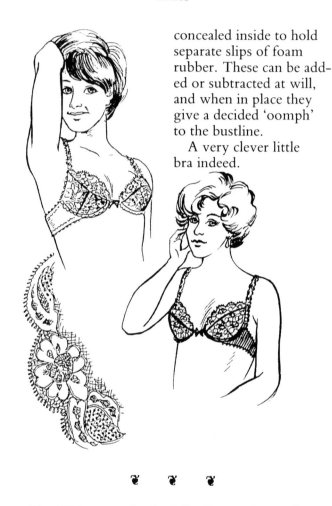

concealed inside to hold separate slips of foam rubber. These can be added or subtracted at will, and when in place they give a decided 'oomph' to the bustline.

A very clever little bra indeed.

❧   ❧   ❧

The 1960s seemed to be full of innovative undies. In about 1967 there came a fashion for 'Cosi-tops' — short, skimpy vests made of stretch Bri-nylon in strong, patterned colours. These were favoured by the young, who often discarded bras completely, and versions of these tops are still around in the 1990s.

There was also an amazing hybrid garment introduced in about 1963 — the bra-slip. At first this could be bought only in pretty pastel shades, but as the clothes of the 1960s progressively shrank into straight, tube-shaped dresses, and as skirts rose to danger-level at the thigh, its colourings became darker and often densely patterned.

In a way, the bra-slip was the last frontier of 'ladylikeness'. The late '60s saw petticoats disappearing fast; tights and mini skirt couldn't cope with a flagging petticoat, and then hot-pants and trousers for women in the 1970s (popular with all ages) made them finally redundant.

The bra-slip I have is a little 'granny print' nylon garment in a black and multi-coloured floral design. It has fibre-filled cups and would have been worn in the heyday of the mini dress. It was made by Etam. We were tremendously keen on bright, flowery patterns in the middle and late 1960s. We also liked so-called 'psychedelic' colours — sharp, searing limes, pinks, oranges and yellows — and a good show of dramatic black and white. Hardly anything pale and interesting could be tracked down in the underwear departments in the high street. Virginal white had to be cornered in old-fashioned drapers' or quieter shopping areas in cathedral towns. The overall look was bold.

Marks & Spencer, alert to trends as usual, marketed a flower-power bra in all-over stretch Lycra; it was brief, with a pink and coral floral design set on a white ground. Doubtless there were pants or a pantie girdle to match. It was a very popular style with young women and I am told, on every occasion I ask, that it was very, very comfortable.

Lycra, of course, is the magic material. It emerged from an involved stable of what is now called 'Elastane'. The first ingredient in its make-up arrived in 1959 with the revolutionary introduction by the American company Du Pont of the fibre Spandex. Then Courtauld's developed Spanzelle. These were both later known as 'elastomerics'. They were power nets and 'Lycra' was the combined result — two man-made fibres, nylon and Spandex.

Flower-power patterns had actually begun to appear, gently, in the late 1950s, but the vogue for full-colour undies was in full swing by the late 1960s, when a universally popular pantie corselette came on the market. Made from figured elastomeric in a bright blue and turquoise floral pattern, it had 'fibrefill' half-lined cups (fibrefill was a soft polyester wadding), high-cut legs, elastic straps with a white lace and ribbon trim. Once more it was a St Michael label.

At the same time as flower power, the 'see through' look —which at first seemed no more than a Press gimmick — set the corsetry business thinking hard.

Sales of traditional products, 'proper' foundation garments and girdles, were falling each season — particularly with younger women who no longer wished to have their bodies shackled behind an elastic fence. The bottom was indeed dropping out of the market. The word 'corset' — a word that had inspired poets and lovers for centuries — was about to become extinct.

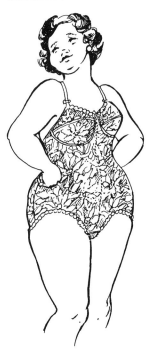

BRAS

At a 'Miss America' pageant in Atlantic City in 1968, feminists burnt their bras as a public demonstration of new-found freedom. Fifty years previously, the bra had stood as a symbol of liberation and female emancipation; now, with this act of defiance, it was viewed by some as an outmoded, male-advocated restriction of a woman's body.

A quiet exile was needed to restore the balance.

Another Diversion
MATERNAL OPENINGS

All women become like their mothers. That is their tragedy . . .
>   *The Importance of Being Earnest.* Oscar Wilde

Having breast-fed five children I feel maternity bras are a subject I can speak on with authority.

The rich, in former centuries — and maybe somewhere even now — could always farm their babies out to 'wet' nurses so that the well-dressed mum of, say, the seventeenth or eighteenth century did not necessarily have to keep hoiking up her dress or unbuckling her stays to feed the baby. By the late eighteenth century enlightenment had begun to glimmer, and the upper classes developed a much warmer attitude towards their little ones. Dresses, which were much simpler in style — often *sans* corsets altogether — were frequently made with slits cut into the bodice or with a separate, plastron front.

This fashion continued into the nineteenth century, and during Victoria's reign 'motherhood' was not only a sweet, admired word but a most noble and wonderful ambition to fulfil. Corsets were designed with adjustable side-lacing, to help mothers overcome the practical problems of suckling their young.

Modern women of this century, and certainly since the 1920s and '30s, have had to rely on a strong cotton, front-fastening bra to see them through this wet patch. A 'nursing' bra usually came with a supply of terry towelling pads. There were also helpful hints to be had from splendid books like *Every Woman's Doctor Book* of 1934. Under the chapter headed 'The New Mother', this practical suggestion is made:

Care of the figure
Many a brand-new mother feels 'all any-how' after she begins to get about again. The full breasts make her feel 'sloppy', and the figure is slack and flabby for the first few weeks.

Here is a hint given me by a nurse. If your figure is not so trim as before owing to the full breasts, make yourself a brassiere from a 45″ length of towelling. Cut it ten or twelve inches wide, and put tiny darts under each breast, and at the underarm seams, to ensure a firm comfortable fitting. The fastening should be at the front, enabling ease for feeding the baby, and narrow shoulder straps will keep the brassiere in position. Many of my patients have found this simple device a great comfort; you will be amazed at the difference such a garment makes to you, and how much more trim and tidy you will feel.

Vintage maternity bras are difficult items to come by — incredibly rare, in fact — so I am lucky to have one made by Southall's, who are possibly best remembered as early manufacturers of sanitary towels, dating from the late 1920s. Made of strong white cotton material with a

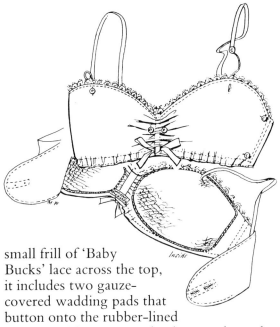

small frill of 'Baby Bucks' lace across the top, it includes two gauze-covered wadding pads that button onto the rubber-lined bodice. Ribbon straps also button through and have four inches of hat elastic attached to 'hold' the garment when the mother is actually feeding the baby.

The bra is shaped under the bust by means of a gathering ribbon which ties centre front, and the back fastens with two buttons.

It is a most cumbersome, fiddly garment and I wonder how many were abandoned by frustrated mums during the first week of use!

It was in the 1930s that, gradually, better support designs for maternity bras became available and major companies started to produce bras with divided cups, a most sensible arrangement.

Firms such as Mothercare, Marks & Spencer and Berlei have always manufactured comfortable maternity underclothes, having researched this area of need for several decades.

Nowadays there are some extremely good, well-made, tough, easily washable maternity bras on the market, so that unbelievable feeling of being blown up like a balloon, with rigid, milk-engorged breasts, is alleviated (it's a time when you would gladly feed four babies at once!). Soluble pads are now seen as the solution to the leakage problem — although I know for a fact that lots and lots of mums still resort to mopping up with a bit of old terry nappy.

No bra, no pad in the world can cope with that initial spurt of milk which so often, perforce, misses the baby's eager lips.

Naturally I speak from experience.

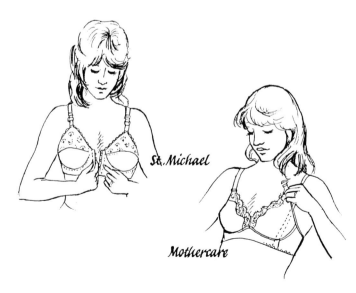

St. Michael

Mothercare

TEN
LET IT ALL HANG OUT

Her bra was pink, his hands were blue
The blasted hooks would not undo!

Anon, 1970

A contemporary journalist has described the Seventies as 'hungover Monday, the day of reckoning after the long weekend (that was the Sixties, that was)'.

Everyone was looking for answers: on religion, health, food, marriage. They sought solutions in mystic gurus, jogging, lentils, divorce. Decimilisation could not disguise terrifying inflation (the £1 of 1970 was worth only 35p by 1979) and prices rose sharply. No wonder 'let's get out of the rat race and live in the sticks with no electricity' became the dream of many.

During the 1970s fashion became disorientated; women looked in fashion magazines and discovered that the thing to do was to wear whatever they liked — provided its qualities were ethnic, flower power, flowing or, best of all, antique. Indeed, the pre-Raph look was definitely in, and Dante Rossetti and Holman Hunt would have found inspiration from thousands of Lizzie Siddal lookalikes.

In the year 1970 the mini skirt was on its last legs. Sizzling hot-pants vied with stair-brushing maxis, while girls who knew a thing or two opted for the discreet charm of the midi skirt, buttoned waist to thigh, exposing the granny-laced knee boots. Zandra Rhodes' lavish, layered semi-transparent dresses caused ripples of amazement across the calm of *haute couture*, while Laura Ashley, fresh, romantic and reminiscent of nicer old days and ways, worked a genteel magic on the better-class high streets.

Overall, the main impression of the Seventies is unisex blue jeans, in various stages of fade, trooping round looking like a crowd of disappointed extras off a Wild West film set. From the back — and often the front — young men and women looked startlingly alike.

Certainly, these girls didn't care a toss about a bra. Rather than go bust, corsetry had to change its image — yet again.

Once more the nudity angle was proffered by manufacturers. Erotic veiling with the 'no wear' underwear was seen as the answer. Seamless bras involved thermo-plastic materials heated to a very high temperature, moulded, cut and then technically assisted to set rapidly. By the mid-1970s many companies were making these will o' the wisp improvements on nature. The stocking-sheer nylon bras were undetectable under the tightest clothes; they were practical, comfortable and easy-care. You could jump on a bus, dance, yoga, do gym, shop or body pop. Stretch straps didn't slip, bra cups didn't cut. It was the most unaware underwear — ever. No one could be certain whether or not you were wearing a bra, even under a T-shirt or silk top, because your nipples were seen in prominent bas-relief . . . particularly on chillier days.

It so happened that, at the time all this *au naturelle* stuff was being hoo-haa'd about, Janet Reger, a superb, imaginative designer, was lavishing her lingerie, including good, old-fashioned, waist-nipping corsets, with frills and furbelows fit for any princess who might happen to set foot inside her shop. She even stocked frilly suspenders — which showed enormous foresight during the decade of neuter tights.

This was the other end of the market — on the one hand plain, practical second skins; on the other, pretty, impractical, lace-bedecked flesh. Time and again this message has been repeated in the history of fashion; women are contrary creatures and like the privilege of changing their minds.

Since Janet Reger rediscovered the thrill of frillies from a design studio in a Paddington backstreet in 1967, there have been other lingerie designers to achieve sensational results in silk with a touch of lace . . . but she was the pioneer. Within ten years she and her husband Peter had opened the doors of their Bond Street shop and, while some women were burning their bras, others sent their men to buy luxury versions for their combined, intimate delight.

Janet Reger has dressed pop stars, film stars and royalty. However, her great genius, which ascended like a lark in the 1970s, plummeted like a dead duck in 1983 when the business was put into liquidation and her trademark sold. I shall never forget the headline in one of the more serious daily newspapers: 'Janet Reger — Business Suspended'.

Happily and most wonderfully, Janet Reger

has regained her distinctive place in the world of fine lingerie. She has a lovely shop in Beauchamp Place, Knightsbridge (or 'Fashion Row' as my London friends call it), and in the last seven years has once again proved what a popular, imaginative designer she is and what a determined creative mind can do even against alarmingly depressing odds.

Beautiful designs still flow from her sketch-pad and she justly deserves her reputation as the Lingerie Queen. Janet Reger is to undies what Hoover is to vacuum cleaners.

Even as imitations of the real thing, silk and lace are still the materials that hold the key to romance — tinged with faint decadence. My 1970s Janet Reger bra is lovely, a scallop shell of cream polyester that shimmers like real satin, trimmed with machine-made lace (which has all the appearance of hand-bobbed Honiton). It is underwired, the cups hinged with material, and has wide-set, lace-covered straps with elastic 'tug' points; the same idea is used for the fastening, which is a hook made from clear plastic.

❧   ❧   ❧

My quest for bras has led me to haunt charity shops and jumble sales, to pester near friends and distant relatives, and even other people's distant relatives.

Once I was stopped in a busy street by a woman who shoved a small parcel into my hands with the words, 'I've got one for you!' I peered into the bag and enthused ecstatically. The woman preened with pleasure and then said, 'I told my husband you'd like it.'

On another occasion I was completely engrossed, sorting through a large tray of bras in a charity shop, when I became aware that the woman standing next to me was regarding me with narrowed eyes as I slung about ten different shapes, sizes and colours to one side with little grunts of satisfaction. Suddenly she could stand it no longer.

'Are you looking for any *particular* sort of bra?' she enquired.

'Oh, no,' I replied, snatching another from the box, 'I like *all* sorts.'

She moved hastily to the other side of the shop.

As a result of these sorties I have acquired several orphans. They are the cast-offs of modern society. Where they came from, who wore them, I do not know; they have all had their day, and there's nothing so old as yesterday's shape. Some have sagged from long use, some are minus a wire, a bit of uplift; one or two are missing a strap, or gone 'yellow' or lost their colour here and there. It doesn't matter, they still contribute to the bra's story.

There are a couple of really Big Girls in this lot, including a splendid cotton Evans outsize, and another beauty in candyfloss pink lace with a 'Lovable' label; and I really care for the famous

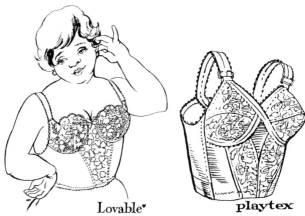

Lovable

playtex

Playtex 'Cross Your Heart' because it always reminds me of the schoolboy rhyme:

> You can't get to Heaven in a Playtex bra
> Cos a Playtex bra won't stretch that far!

There is also a splendid little T-shirt bra with a 'racer' back that fastens in the front. This device is one that an elegant, model-girl friend refers to as a 'front loader'.

I have to admit there are also some very odd bras in my collection. One, catalogued as 'Soho', is a black acetate satin and Lycra-panelled basque with seven cased bones and four suspenders, the whole thing trimmed with black lace. Quite conventional — apart from the upper region which is non-existent. The bust area, the cups, are simply not there — but the bustline is underwired with extremely rigid steels. It looks extraordinary, like something from Ancient Crete. This piece of erotica would have shoved the boobs aloft in a prodigious and, possibly, most uncomfortable manner. The label states only that it is English made.

Well, well...

Another strange little bra, made of white nylon and elastic, is nothing more than a narrow shelf

— an underwired quarter-bra which is shaped, most skilfully, to form an upward-thrusting band around the breasts. It is beautifuly made and finished. The label reads, 'Odette. Continental. Made in England' (which sounds at cross-purposes).

And, finally, a wonderful white twilled cotton bra with cased bones running vertically through the cups and decorated with massive silver sequins. This bra belonged to a show girl and was part of a costume in the late 1930s. The dancer's name, Sheila, is marked inside, and, heavily underlined, 'ACT II. CURTAIN'.

This bra is a proto-type of the popular, decorated bras of the 1990s.

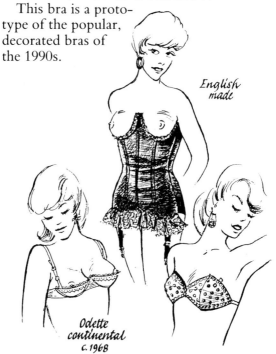

English made

Odette continental c.1968

ELEVEN
ART VERSUS NATURE

All passes. Art alone
   Enduring stays to us;
The Bust outlasts the throne . . .
   Ars Victrix. Henry Austin Dobson

The 1980s taught women to look after themselves and tried to convince them that they should be seen as the successful species. Never mind if, in private, they were uncertain, depressed, fearing for the future, caught in unstable relationships with indifferent or uncontrollable children; in public they must be seen to cope. Eighties woman had to be independent and clever: good job, a good home, good social life, good taste and good health. Indeed, health became an obsessive interest. Fashion editors spoke knowingly of 'body consciousness', and lots of healthy exercise was promoted to give you a nice, strong, Eighties–style body. So–called 'Power Dressing' helped women look confident and in command, even if, deep down, they felt neither.

The 'big' bosom came back into fashion, accompanied by a craze for hefty padded shoulders (a re-run of Elsa Schiaparelli's famous 'square' look of the late 1930s) inspired by TV 'soaps' such as *Dynasty* and *Dallas*.

The new, Boadicea bosom did not necessarily need a bra to go with it. Voluptuous model girls often owed more to cosmetic surgery than they did to wire and padding; an implant can stand up for itself. Self-reliant boobs were shown off in 'tubes' — circles of stretch material — while the British designer Vivienne Westwood, the Japanese Issey Miyake and the French Jean-Paul Gaultier all provided extraordinary, deviant shapes for the female torso.

Gaultier, in 1984, celebrated the return of en-
larged breasts by fixing eight-inch cones to the
chest of a corset-like evening dress. Miyake used
body-moulded rubber to make a bustier that
erotically held the breasts like a silicone sculp-
ture. Westwood flirted with punk, with bodice-
ripped bondage, with leather and eventually, in
1990, with a seventeenth-century style corset,
worn as Arcadian outerwear (not at all a new idea
since aristocrats had worn decorated corsets outside their dresses centuries before). These Westwood fantasies squeezed the breasts into the sort
of sensuous orbs that would have had the poet
Robert Herrick reaching for quill and ink. The
luscious, teasing image has remained a preoccu-
pation of the designer.

In the end, the most important thing is to sell
the goods. To do that you've got to let the customer know about it. It doesn't matter if it is
kitchen equipment, motor cars, houses, holidays
— or bras. Advertising and marketing them is
essential; no market, no trade. The simplicity of
Michael Marks' small card in the 1880s is now
somewhat overshadowed by the sophisticated
selling techniques used to promote merchandise.

Leading bra manufacturers such as Triumph
International spend millions of pounds advertising their products in newspapers, on display
posters, point-of-sale photographs, packaging
and, essentially, in women's magazines.

Triumph was founded in Germany in 1886 by
the Spiesshofer and Braun families, who are still
actively involved in its management. The British
operation started in 1964 and now employs 500

people in two factories. They design and manufacture some of the most beautiful and popular bras seen today.

Triumph pioneered in the 1970s the technique of moulding fabric to form bust cups. Machines, unique to Triumph, were designed and built by their own engineers, and even delicate, lacy fabrics can now be moulded to a beautiful fit for garments including, not only bras, but briefs, slips, camisoles and bodyshapers, from energetic styles to the decidedly romantic.

The bosom has long been exposed by the popular Press. The camera has recorded breasts bared and breasts barely concealed. Such treatment often treads a thin line between allure and depravity. It's the old story — what one culture, one group of people deem high fashion, another will scornfully dismiss as ridiculous.

In 1986 a male fashion student conceived the female shape clothed in strident terms of a black seamed leather jerkin, tightly zipped, with terrifyingly pointed copper breasts! This garment owes much to the images cast by science fiction and demonic Hell's Angels, subconsciously invoking the grotesque drawing of 'woman' portrayed as 'the Devil' in an illuminated manuscript done by a twelfth-century monk.

Nowadays fashion — over and under — is a very sophisticated industry. It is also volatile. What bra to wear is a personal choice, not a social dictate as it once appeared to be ; now women can have all their options left open.

So, the girl who has tried everything from bustiers to bodyshapers might fancy a 'candy bra'. This sweetie, a product of Cosmorotics Inc, comes with its matching panties in a design called 'Tea Cups,' and is flavoured, a lip-smacking liquorice. It's what is known as a tit-bit.

Or a recent exposure is the new kind of self-adhesive bra, 'Joli'bust' of Paris. Take two shaped pieces of sticky plastic, fix them beneath your breasts, and there you go, a perfectly real you with (temporarily) enhanced curves. Women who have tried them say they're 'wonderful', particularly under sheer blouses or breath-catching evening clothes.

They were first marketed in the mid-eighties and they come with a set of simple instructions on how to use, with a note that it is best not to remove while the skin is damp.

You are warned: no sweat-making activity before undressing.

For those with a yen for sensationalism, what about this: two elliptical curves of black nylon decorated with gold embroidery on a halter elastic strap — it's that erotic teaser, a nipple-less bra.

It is French, naturally enough, and I bought it one dreary, rain-soaked afternoon after I had been surveying the bra-buying scene in dozens of department stores and high street multiples. It came from a select Knightsbridge lingerie shop, not a stone's throw from Harvey Nichols. There it was in the window, enticingly displayed with others of its kind, for all the world to see. Indeed, the whole window was a stunning revelation.

Rose Lewis, who started the shop thirty years ago, is now dead, but it is run by her two assistants and the style is still a touch old-fashioned — not bright, modern and transitory but velvety, quiet and everlasting. You are certainly not rushed at Rose Lewis.

The merchandise is all somewhat specialist, including made-to-measure corsetry; it is in the luxury class. A good deal of the lingerie on show is French, some of it lavishly trimmed or incredibly daring. It is also incredibly expensive. The tiny open-plan bra cost £60 — goodness knows what price it would be without the holes!

TWELVE
BLOOMING BIG

No one can deny the boost that Madonna has
given the bra. This unique, American entertainer
— dancer, singer, actress — is the vital embodi-
ment of western Pop culture. Her nurture in the
United States during the past 30 years is the
mainspring for her excess of raunchy, confron-
tational sex appeal. She would have been raised
amid the continuous sound of rock/pop music,
blaring out from competitive, commercial radio
stations twenty-four hours a day.

Madonna is already a cult
legend and she has riveting dress
style: a 'Barbie' doll come to life,
a woman who has stepped
straight out of a strip
cartoon. She could wear a
dustbin and still generate
steamy, sexual excitement.

As it is, Jean-Paul
Gaultier has been the
dynamic force behind
the inspired, infamous,
bust-projecting corset
costumes worn in her
films, videos and stage

shows. When she wore his hard, conical bra during her 'Blonde Ambition' tour of 1990, a style he had designed years before, its emotive power was suddenly etched into the public consciousness.

Here, then, is the real source of influence for underwear worn as outerwear that we have witnessed since the mid-1980s. Those jumble sale 'English Rose' bras or bizarrely decorated bustiers worn over T-shirts or skinny vests by young girls are a watered-down version of the amazing Madonna's impact as a 'Power-Undresser'.

The much publicised 'Bullet Bra' was a design concept initiated by the renowned *corsetières*, Rigby and Peller, who since 1952 have held the Royal Warrant from the Queen. The Bullet Bra was based on an antique breastplate worn by Italian soldiers, intimidating and protective at one and the same time.

Rigby and Peller have made superbly fitted, bespoke bras and corsets for aristocrats, actresses and major and minor royalty since they started business in 1939. Their first premises were in South Molton Street, but during the 1980s — and the bosom revival — the showroom and small workforce were moved to the hub of well-heeled shopping in Hans Road, Knightsbridge. Rigby and Peller are to bras what Rolls Royce is to motor-cars, and they still make the wonderful waist-cinchers and basques which they were making when Mrs Rigby and Mrs Peller first arrived in England from Vienna.

The company is now owned by Mr and Mrs Kenton who have a long experience of the corsetry business, and the workmanship and beauty of their heirloom garments is as fine as ever. Modern 'young things' still go to have their waists whittled down and their bosoms moulded into a 'nice, curvaceous look', just as their mothers did before them.

Mrs Kenton showed me a magnificent 'Madonna'-inspired corset made of jet-black, cotton-backed satin, with six cased and velvet-ended

bones set into the structure. The extremely pointed cups are stiffly interlined and then top-stitched by hand in yellow thread. There are similarly stitched inserts flaring over the hips of the basque, and the stomacher front is a double-busk of cased leather punched through and 'eye-leted' with gilt heart-shapes and criss-crossed with a gilt chain. The shoulder-straps are wide, non-slip satin ribbon and the back of the corset fastens with a double flank of 16 hooks and eyes.

It is a compelling, must-be-looked-at garment, designed as outrageous, show-off outer-wear; not, perhaps, the sort of thing for a shrinking violet to contemplate.

Janet Reger's 1991 range included a stunner in black and white — a half-bra made of real silk satin set off by a flourish of dramatic black lace in a bold, vaguely 1940s, floral pattern.

The bra is edged with fine black lace trims and the narrow shoulder-straps are also lace-covered. It fastens at the back with a hook-and-eye sewn on a silk-covered elastic 'tug'. It is the kind of sexy but sweet item of lingerie that lots of women secretly wish to possess — and would dearly love as an intimate gift from 'him'.

Most women, however, wear a bra from Marks & Spencer. Top of the 1991 range, and incorporating the fine plissé pleating that was a feature of swish, up-market bras during the year, was a cream, stretch lace and pleated satin, underwired bra — called, appropriately enough, 'Fortuny Pleat'.

It is beautifully made with lace ruffles stitched on the elasticated straps and a triple bar of hooks and eyes.

Although this bra has a

St Michael label, it could have been manufactured by one of the leading corsetry companies
within the British Isles, which are contracted to
produce a percentage of their goods bearing the
M&S label.

Triumph have produced an elegant 'body' in a
stunning white stretch lace, patterned with enormous swirling flowers reminiscent of Victorian
parlour curtains. A show-stopper!

The 'body' is definitely 'the business' for the
continuing '90s as seen by the vast American
mail-order company Victoria's Secret. Its beautiful catalogue is chock-full of delicious undies —
sexy or svelte — including a sensational olive
green panné velvet bodysuit, described as an 'un-
expected choice' for lingerie.

Some British mail-order firms have problems!
A 42C bra was returned with a note from the
agent which read: 'Does not fit. Customer wants
to exchange for pillow-cases'.

A letter in the 1960s archives of the Silhouette
company, from an Irishwoman, bears witness to
the religious significance of colour:

> I don't know what possessed me to do it but
> on Tuesday I bought some of your black
> underwear, the Magic Moments Pantee
> Corselet, to be precise. I have never worn
> black undergarments before in my life and
> you can believe me when I say that I will
> never do so again. The day I wore it for the
> first time, which was the day before yester-
> day, when I got undressed in the evening I
> found that I had come out in a rash. I knew

Triumph

Passionata

at once that I was being punished for my sinfulness. I prayed to the Good Lord for forgiveness and have been to confession and the Priest said that he hoped that God in his infinite mercy would forgive me this transgression, provided I was truly penitent and would never again harbour such thoughts that would prompt me to do such a thing. I hope so much that this will prove true, although as yet the rash does not look to be clearing up.

PS. I enclose the corselet and in view of the fact that it has barely been worn I am sure you will see your way clear to refund me the purchase price.

Today, however, the underwear department in any large store displays bras (coloured or virgin white) for every shape, size, structure or occasion, beautiful with breastfuls of lace or fit and bouncy in youthful stretch fabric.

❦   ❦   ❦

Fashion travels many avenues to arrive at a destination. What one generation scorns another will praise to the skies. However art-conscious or 'way-out', clothes, at some stage, have to fit round a basic anatomy. A garment has to be worn. Helen Storey is a young London couturier whose work is a mixture of art and wearability. She admits 'an emotional response' to having been, as a teenager, 'a skinhead by day and a ballet student by night'. Her designs have an intrinsic sculptural element that is both functional and decorative. For 1991 she attached outer-wear, whirlpool-stitched bras of heavy cord to her minimalist tube dresses.

Vivienne Westwood, British Designer of the Year for 1990 and 1991 and one of the more controversial designers of our time, continues to love the corset look. There have been few fashion originators in the past hundred years, and three of the finest have been women —

Coco Chanel, Mary Quant and Vivienne Westwood.

Her thoroughly intellectual and historical approach to her work is evident in her sensational corset, called 'Boule', made of gleaming red satin Lycra and stiff with strip-plastic boning. A majestic motif of hand-stencilled orb and oak tree is applied in gold. It is thought-provoking stuff — why on earth would a fashion designer of the 1990s wish to put women back into corsets?

It has been said that every time fashion gets really stuck into showing off the bosom it heralds some catastrophic event or change in society. The onset of war, recession or political upheaval seems to bring out the breast in women. Perhaps it is because, at these crucial times, the latent Earth Mother takes over and a psychological need to nourish is further induced.

In the 1990s, with economic tedium and a falling birth-rate forecast, this adage seems to be holding up. Waists are in, bosoms, bless 'em, are out. Paris is passionate about big, beautiful breasts; so are Italy and America, and model girls are only welcome if they can fill a 34B cup — preferably more.

What is bad news for ardent feminists, even with a ferociously liberated leader like Madonna, is extremely happy news for bra manufacturers. This decade is tipped to produce blockbuster business for them.

Maybe, as sex becomes an increasingly risky transaction, women will flaunt their erogenous zones but remain dominant, displaying not so much their soft, yielding bodies as their tough, sardonic minds.

Whatever comes to pass it will be interesting, and the bra will have come a long, long way from fig leaves — or has it?

BIBLIOGRAPHY

Costume in Detail, Nancy Bradfield. George Harrap & Co, 1968.

A History of Costume in the West, Francois Boucher. Thames & Hudson, 1967.

Dress and Undress, Elizabeth Ewing. Batsford, 1978.

The History of Underclothes, C. Willett and Phillis Cunnington. Faber, 1951.

Fashion in Underwear, Elizabeth Ewing. Batsford, 1971.

A History of Women's Underwear, Cecil Saint-Laurent. Academy Editions, 1986.

Dress and Morality, Aileen Ribeiro. Batsford, 1986.

'Le Corset', Ernest Leoty. 1893.

English Women's Clothing in the Present Century, C. Willett Cunnington. Faber & Faber, 1952.

And All Was Revealed, Doreen Caldwell. Arthur Barker, 1981.

The Handbook of English Costume in the Eighteenth Century, C. Willett and Phillis Cunnington. Faber & Faber, 1957.

Corsets and Crinolines, Norah Waugh. Batsford, 1954.

The Habits of Good Society, by a Gentleman and a Matron of Society. James Hogg and Son, 1859.

Foundations of Fashion, Christopher Page. Leicestershire Museums, 1981.

OTHER SOURCES

Home Chat, Volumes I–II, 1895.

The Girl's Own Paper, 1897.

The Lady of 1898, 1901, 1935 and 1936.

The Modern Woman. Associated Newspapers Ltd, c1937.

Every Woman's Book of Health and Beauty. The Amalgamated Press Ltd, c 1935.

Vogue, from 1937–1991.

Everywoman, *Woman*, *Woman's Own* and *Honey* magazines, 1957–1975.